Colombia

The Genocidal Democracy

Javier Giraldo, S.J.

Common Courage Press   Monroe, Maine

Cover design by Matt Wuerker and Doug Alexander
Cover photo by Herney Patiño, *Colombia Hoy* and *Cambio 16*
Map by Zoltan Grossman

Library of Congress Cataloging-in-Publication Data
Giraldo, Javier.
Colombia : the genocidal democracy / Javier Giraldo.
p. cm.
Includes index.
ISBN 1-56751-086-8 (alk. paper). -- ISBN 1-56751-087-6
1. State-sponsored terrorism--Colombia. 2. Victims of state-sponsored terrorism--Colombia. 3. Armed forces--Political activity.
4. Assassinations--Colombia. 5. Human rights--Colombia.
6. Colombia--Politics and government--1974- I. Title.
HV6433.C6G57   1996
323.4'9'09861-dc20   9614341
CIP

Common Courage Press
Box 702
Monroe, ME 04951

207-525-0900   fax: 207-525-3068

First Printing

Contents

Colombia

✹ Massacre site   ⊙ Paramilitary headquarters

★ Capital city   • Other city

0   100   200 miles

Caribbean Sea

GUAJIRA

Barranquilla   • Santa Marta

Cartagena

PANAMA

CÓRDOBA   • Cúcuta

VENEZUELA

Barranca-bermeja

URABÁ   • Bucaramanga

Apartadó

Puerto Berrío   SANTANDER

San Vicente de Chucurí

Medellín   BOYACÁ

Puerto Boyacá   CASANARE

Cauca

Manizales

PACIFIC OCEAN

Pereira   Bogotá

Trujillo

Ibagué   Villavicencio

Buenaventura

Riofrío   META

Magdalena

Cali   GUAINÍA

Neiva

Santander de Quilichao

CAUCA

• Florencia

CAQUETÁ

ECUADOR

BRAZIL

Putumayo

Amazon

PERU   *Amazon*

Zoltán Grossman,
Wisconsin Cartographers' Guild,
Tel./Fax (608) 246-2256

Acknowledgments

In May of 1994, some Jesuits from Fundacion Luis Espinal, in Barcelona, Spain, generously offered me space in their booklet *Cristianism i Justicia* in order to give a testimony about death in my country, as part of the framework of a campaign for the respect of the most basic human rights in Colombia, which is supported by numerous humanitarian organizations. To my fellow Jesuits my fraternal gratitude.

Edited in September of 1994, the booklet started to reach the most unsuspected places by mail. In January of 1995, one of our collaborators with the Comision de Justicia y Paz, the Canadian journalist Daniel Bland, showed me an English version of the piece. Due to his long experience in Colombia, he able to recognize in the text some interpretations that this tragic reality showed. Unbeknownst to me, he had translated the work, with the idea of spreading it to English speaking countries.

Daniel's interest quickly coincided with that of Cecilia Zárate, who along with her husband, attorney John Laun, had started their own translation process in Madison, Wisconsin. John very generously took time from his busy schedule to translate the whole piece on paramilitarism. When I thank these friends for their work, above all I want to recognize their refined solidarity with the victims, who in our country do not have recognition even for their most elementary dignity as human beings.

At the beginning of June, 1995, I received another suprise. At Cecilia's request, Professor Noam Chomsky, for whom I have had deep respect for many years, had generously written a preface for the English edition. I found this to be an excessive honor, but at the same time

I recognize in his gesture something that shows his characteristic greatness: his enormous capacity to discover and unveil the insanity of the powerful and to ponder their monstrosity when he examines them from the perspective of the suffering humble ones.

My gratitude goes also to Blase Bonpane, who from Los Angeles suggested to Cecilia that she contact Common Courage Press in Maine, to get support in the urgency of telling our story in the U.S. Very specially I want to thank my editor at Common Courage, Greg Bates, for all his patience, generosity and understanding during this process which was difficult to coordinate, being worked on in distant cities simultaneously. But above everything to Greg, for believing in the importance of telling the truth, a basic premise in a democracy.

I also want to extend my gratitude to Ms. Jean Lepisto for typing the manuscript on paramilitarism, giving her time generously from her work at the law office.

I extend my acknowledgments also to Mr. Steven Kellner, who harnessed modern computer technology in the service of the project. These two people showed fine feelings of solidarity.

Without the human values of friendship and affection that all of these gestures express, I recognize that their primary objective is to spread the outcry of a people horribly victimized who give them the credit for an acknowledgment which I express here in the name of so many thousands of victims and from those who share with them teir tragedy.

Javier Giraldo Moreno, S.J.
Santafe de Bogata, April 1996

Introduction

The Culture of Fear

Two facts should be uppermost in the minds of North American readers of Father Giraldo's documentation of the reign of terror that engulfed Colombia during the "Dirty War" waged by the state security forces and their paramilitary associates from the early 1980s. The first is that Colombia's "democra-tatorship," as Eduardo Galeano termed this amalgam of democratic forms and totalitarian terror, has managed to compile the worst human rights record in the hemisphere in recent years, no small achievement when one considers the competition. The second is that Colombia has had accessories in crime, primary among them the government of the United States, though Britain, Israel, Germany, and others have also helped to train and arm the assassins and torturers of the narco-military-landowner network that maintains "stability" in a country that is rich in promise, and a nightmare for many of its people.

In July 1989, the U.S. State Department announced plans for subsidized sales of military equipment to Colombia, allegedly "for antinarcotics purposes." The sales were "justified" by the fact that "Colombia has a democratic form of government and does not exhibit a consistent pattern of gross violations of internationally recognized human rights." A few months before, the Commission of Justice and Peace that Father Giraldo heads had published a report documenting atrocities in the first part of 1988, including over 3,000 politically-motivated killings, 273 in "social cleansing" campaigns. Political killings averaged eight a day, with seven people murdered in their homes or in the street and one "disappeared." Citing this report, the Washington Office on Latin America (WOLA) added that "the vast majority of those who have disappeared in recent years are grassroots organizers, peasant or union leaders, leftist politicians, human rights workers and other activists," over 1500 by the time of the State Department's praise for Colombia's democracy and its respect for human rights. During the 1988 electoral campaigns, 19 of 87 mayoral candidates of the sole independent political party, the UP were assassinated, along with over 100 of its other candidates. The Central Organization of Workers, a coalition of trade unions formed in 1986, had by then lost over 230 members, most of them found dead after brutal torture.

But the "democratic form of government" emerged without stain, and with no "consistent pattern of gross violations" of human rights.

By the time of the State Department's report, the practices it found praiseworthy were being more efficiently implemented. Political killings in 1988 and 1989 rose to 11 a day, the Colombian branch of the Andean Commission of Jurists reported. From 1988 through early 1992, 9,500 people were assassinated for political reasons along with 830 disappearances and 313 massacres (between 1988 and 1990) of peasants and poor people.

Throughout these years, as usual, the primary victims of state terror were peasants. In 1988, grassroots organizations in one southern department reported a "campaign of total annihilation and scorched earth, Vietnam-style," conducted by the military forces "in a most criminal manner, with assassinations of men, women, elderly and children. Homes and crops are burned, obligating the peasants to leave their lands."

Also in 1988 the government of Colombia established a new judicial regime that called for "total war against the internal enemy." It authorized "maximal criminalization of the political and social opposition," a European-Latin American Inquiry reported in Brussels, reviewing "the consolidation of state terror in Colombia."

As the State Department report appeared a year after these events, the Colombian Minister of Defense again articulated the doctrine of "total war" by state power "in the political, economic, and social arenas." Guerrillas were the official targets, but as a high military official had observed in 1987, their organizations were of minor importance: "the real danger," he explained, is "what the insurgents have called the political and psychological war," the efforts "to control the popular elements" and "to manipulate the masses." The subversives" hope to influence unions, universities, media, and so on, and the government must counter this "war" with its own "total war in the political, economic, and social arenas." Reviewing doctrine and practice, the Brussels study concludes realistically that the "internal enemy" of the state terrorist apparatus extends to "labor organizations, popular movements, indigenous organizations, oppositional political parties, peasant movements, intellectual sectors, religious currents, youth and student groups, neighborhood organizations," indeed any group that must be secured against undesirable influences. "Every individual who in one or another manner supports the goals of the enemy must be considered a traitor and treated in that manner," a Colombian military manual prescribes.

The manual dates from 1963. At that time, violence in Colombia was coming to be "exacerbated by external factors," the president of the Colombian Permanent

Committee for Human Rights, former Minister of Foreign Affairs Alfredo Vásquez Carrizosa, wrote some years later, reviewing the outcome. "During the Kennedy administration," he continues, Washington "took great pains to transform our regular armies into counterinsurgency brigades, accepting the new strategy of the death squads." These initiatives "ushered in what is known in Latin America as the National Security Doctrine,...not defense against an external enemy, but a way to make the military establishment the masters of the game...[with] the right to combat the internal enemy, as set forth in the Brazilian doctrine, the Argentine doctrine, the Uruguayan doctrine, and the Colombian doctrine: it is the right to fight and to exterminate social workers, trade unionists, men and women who are not supportive of the establishment, and who are assumed to be communist extremists."

The "Dirty War" escalated in the early 1980s—not only in Colombia—as the Reagan administration extended these programs throughout the region, leaving it devastated, strewn with hundreds of thousands of corpses tortured and mutilated people who might otherwise have been insufficiently supportive of the establishment, perhaps even influenced by "subversives."

North Americans should never allow themselves to forget the origins of "the Brazilian doctrine, the Argentine doctrine, the Uruguayan doctrine, the Colombian doctrine," and others like them. They were crafted right, then adapted by students trained and equipped right here. The basic guidelines are spelled out in U.S. manuals of counterinsurgency and "low intensity conflict." These are euphemisms, technical terms for state terror, a fact well known in Latin America. When Archbishop Oscar Romero wrote to President Carter in

1980 shortly before his assassination, vainly pleading with him to end U.S. support for the state terrorist, he informed the rector of the Jesuit University, Father Ellacuría, that he was prompted "by the new concept of special warfare, which consists in murderously eliminating every endeavor of the popular organizations under the allegation of Communism or terrorism...." So Father Ellacuría reported shortly before he was assassinated by the same hands a decade later; the events framed the murderous decade with symbolism as gruesome as it was appropriate.

The agents of state terror are the beneficiaries of U.S. training designed to ensure that they have an "understanding of, and orientation toward, U.S. objectives," Defense Secretary Robert McNamera informed National Security Adviser McGeorge Bundy in 1965. This is a matter of particular importance "in the Latin American cultural environment," where it is recognized that the military must be prepared to "remove government leaders from office, whenever, in the judgment of the military, the conduct of these leaders is injurious to the welfare of the nation." It is the right of the military and those who provide them with the proper orientation who are entitled to determine the welfare of the nation, not the beasts of burden toiling and suffering and expiring in their own lands.

When the State Department announced new arms shipments as a reward for Colombia's achievements in human rights and democracy, it surely had access to the record of atrocities that had been compiled by the leading international and Colombian human rights organizations. It was also fully aware of the U.S. role in establishing and maintaining the regime of terror and oppression. The example is, unfortunately, typical of a pattern that hardly varies, as can be readily verified.

As the "Dirty War" of the 1980s took its ever more grisly toll, U.S. participation increased. From 1984 through 1992, 6,844 Colombian soldiers were trained under the U.S. international Military Education and Training Program. Over 2,000 Colombian officers were trained from 1990 to 1992, as "violence reached unprecedented levels" during the presidency of César Gaviria, WOLA reported, confirming conclusions of international human rights monitors.

President Gaviria was a particular favorite of Washington, so admired that the Clinton administration imposed him as Secretary-General of the Organization of American States in a power play that aroused much resentment. "He has been very forward looking in building democratic institutions in a country where it was sometimes dangerous to do so," the U.S. representative to the OAS explained—not inquiring into the reasons for the "dangers," however. The training program for Colombian officers is the largest in the hemisphere, and U.S. military aid to Colombia now amounts to about half the total for the entire hemisphere. It has increased under Clinton, Human Rights Watch reports, adding that he planned to turn to emergency overdrawing facilities when the Pentagon did not suffice for still further increases.

The official cover story for the participation in crime is the war "against the guerrillas and narcotrafficking operations." In its 1989 announcement of new arms sales, the State Department could rely on its human rights reports, which attributed virtually all violence to the guerrillas and narcotraffickers. Hence the U.S. is "justified" in providing military equipment and training for the mass murderers and torturers. A month later, George Bush announced the largest shipment of arms ever authorized under the emergency provisions of the

Foreign Assistance Act. The arms were not sent to the National Police, which is responsible for almost all counter-narcotic operations, but to the army. The helicopters and jet planes are useless for the drug war, as was pointed out at once, but not for other purposes. Human rights groups soon reported bombing of villages and other atrocities. It is also impossible to imagine that Washington is not aware that the security forces it is maintaining are closely linked to the narcotrafficking operations, and that exactly as their leaders frankly say, the target is the "internal enemy" that might support or be influenced by "subversives" in some way.

A January 1994 conference on state terror organized by Jesuits in San Salvador observed that "it is important to explore...what weight the culture of terror has had in domesticating the expectations of the majority vis-a-vis alternatives different to those of the powerful." That is the crucial point, wherever such methods are used to subdue the "internal enemy." Israeli physician Ruchama Marton, who has been at the forefront of investigation of the use of torture by the security forces of her own country, points out that while confessions obtained by torture are of course meaningless, the real purpose is not confession. Rather, it is silence, "silence induced by fear." "Fear is contagious," she continues, "and spreads to the other members of the oppressed group, to silence and paralyze them. To impose silence through violence is torture's real purpose, in the most profound and fundamental sense." The same is true of all other aspects of the doctrines that have been devised and implemented with our guidance and support under a series of fraudulent guises.

To impose silence on the internal enemy is necessary in the "democra-tatorships" that U.S. policy has sought to impose on its domains ever since it "assumed, out of self-interest, responsibility for the welfare of the world capitalist system," in the words of diplomatic Gerald Haines, senior historian of the CIA, discussing the U.S. takeover of Brazil in 1945—and indeed before, with important echoes at home as well. It is particularly important to impose silence in the region with the highest inequality in the world, thanks in no small measure to policies of the superpower that largely controls it. It is necessary to impose silence and spread fear in countries like Colombia, where the top three percent of the landed elite own over 70% of arable land while 57% of the poorest farmers subsist on under 3%—a country where 40% of the population live in "absolute poverty," unable to satisfy basic subsistence needs according to an official government report in 1986, and 18% live in "absolute misery," unable to meet nutritional needs. The Colombian Institute of Family Welfare estimates that four and a half million children under 14 are hungry, half the country's children. Recall that we are speaking of a country of enormous resources and potential. It has "one of the healthiest and most flourishing economies in Latin America," Latin Americanist John Martz writes in Current History, lauding this triumph of capitalism in a society with "democratic structures" which, "notwithstanding inevitable flaws, are among the most solid on the continent," a model of "well-established political stability"—conclusions that are not inaccurate, if not quite in the sense he seeks to convey.

The effects of U.S. arms and military training are not confined to Colombia. The record of horrors is all too full. In the Jesuit journal *America*, Rev. Daniel Santiago, a priest working in El Salvador, reported in 1990 the story of a peasant woman who returned home one day to find her mother, sister, and three children sitting around a table, the decapitated head of each person placed on the table in front of the body, the hands arranged on top "as if each body was stroking its own head." The assassins, from the Salvadoran National Guard, had found it hard to keep the head of an 18-month-old baby in place, so they nailed the hands to it. A large plastic bowl filled with blood stood in the center of the table. Two years earlier, the Salvadoran human rights group that continued to function despite the assassination of its founders and directors reported that 13 bodies had been found in the preceding two weeks, most showing signs of torture, including two women who had been hanged from a tree by their hair, their breasts cut off and their faces painted red. The discoveries were familiar, but the timing is significant, just as Washington was successfully completing the cynical exercise of exempting its murderous clients from the terms of the Central America peace accords that called for "justice, freedom and democracy," "respect for human rights," and guarantees for "the endless inviolability of all forms of life and liberty." The record is endless, and endlessly shocking.

Such macabre scenes, which rarely reached the mainstream in the United States, are designed for intimidation. Father Santiago writes that "People are not just killed by death squads in El Salvador—they are decapitated and then their heads are placed on pikes and used to dot the landscape. Men are not just disemboweled by the Salvadoran Treasury Police; their severed genitalia are stuffed in their mouths. Salvadoran women are not just raped by the National Guard; their wombs are cut from their bodies and used to cover their faces. It is not enough to kill children; they are dragged over barbed wire until the flesh falls from their bones while parents are forced to watch." "The aesthetics of terror in El

Salvador is religious." The intention is to ensure that the individual is totally subordinated to the interests of the Fatherland, which is why the death squads are sometimes called the "Army of National Salvation" by the governing ARENA party.

The same is true in neighboring Guatemala. In the traditional "culture of fear," Latin American scholar Piero Gleijeses writes, peace and order were guaranteed by ferocious repression, and its contemporary counterpart follows the same course: "Just as the Indian was branded a savage beast to justify his exploitation, so those who sought social guerrillas, or terrorists, or drug dealers, or whatever the current term of art may be. The fundamental reason, however, is always the same: the savage beast may fall under the influence of "subversives" who challenge the regime of injustice, oppression and terror that must continue to serve the interests of foreign investors and domestic privilege.

Throughout these grim years, nothing has been more inspiring than the courage and dedication of those who have sought to expose and overcome the culture of fear in their suffering countries. They have left martyrs, whose voices have been silenced by the powerful—yet another crime. But they continue to struggle on. Father Giraldo's remarkable work and eloquent words should not only inspire us, but also impel us to act to bring these terrors to an end, as we can. His testimony here contains an "urgent appeal." It should be answered, but it does not go far enough. Our responsibilities extend well beyond. The fate of Colombians and many others hinges on our willingness and ability to recognize and meet them.

—Noam Chomsky
Cambridge, MA
May 1995

Victims of Political Violence in Colombia, 1988—1995

Political Assassinations	6,177
Assassinations Presumed to be Political	10,556
Assassinations Presumed to be "Social Cleansing"	2,459
Deaths in Combat between Army and Guerrillas	9,140
People Forcibly Disappeared	1,451
Obscure Assassinations*	37,595
Total:	67,378
Average per month	701.9
Average per day	23.4

Source: Data Bank of the Comision Inter-Congregacional de Justicia y Paz.

The Inter-Congregational Commission of Peace and Justice, is an umbrella-like organization made up of more than 55 Catholic Religious Orders spread all over the country. Father Javier Giraldo S.J. is its executive director.

*Note: By "Obscure Assassinations" is meant killings for which no motive has clearly been identified when the murder was registered. The killings in this classification do not, however, include those committed for personal problems such as fights or revenge, nor the victims of common crimes committed by private persons.

The importance of this category lies in the fact that on occasion assassinations initially classified as "obscure" are later placed in the category of "political assassinations," or assassinations for "social cleansing," as information later compiled clarifies the motive, the person or persons responsible, or both.

Political Killings: A Regional Comparison

Country	# of years under military dictatorship	# of political killings
Uruguay	16	220
Argentina	8	9,000
Brazil	15	125
Bolivia	17	243
Chile	17	2,666

Colombian "democracy":

President Barco (1986-1990)	13,635
President Gaviria (1990-1994)	14,856
Victims of political violence in Colombia January 1988 to June 1995	28,332

Source: Data bank of the Comision Inter-Congregacional de Justicia y Paz.

Behind the Stereotype
Human Rights in Colombia

1. The Making of a Stereotype

In the spring of 1986, I was invited by the Catholic Development Committee Against Hunger to take part in the Lenten celebration in France. Before I began to speak, I asked members of the audience what kind of images they associated with my country. Invariably, they associated Colombia with drugs, coffee, cyclists (the annual Tour de France bicycle race is held there) and volcanos (where the November 1985 tragedy of Armero took place, a small town in Colombia that was almost totally buried by an avalanche).

There is no doubt that drugs are the first thing that come to people's minds when they think of Colombia. Some have attributed 80% of the world's drug trade to the Colombian cartels. Although I think the problem has been somewhat blown out of proportion, given the fact that the clandestine nature of the business makes accurate estimates difficult to come by, there is no denying its magnitude. What is important is that this perspective has resulted in the false conclusion that violence in Colombia is linked to drug traffic. Is this simply a result of investigative laziness or are there other factors involved?

Consider the following. On January 30, 1993, a car bomb exploded on a downtown street in Bogota killing 20 people. Almost immediately, news of the bomb, which was attributed to drug traffickers, was circulated worldwide by international press agencies. During the same month of January, 1993, our human rights data bank registered 134 cases of political murder and 16 cases of enforced disappearance in the country.

- In 25 of the murders and 6 of the disappearances all indications suggested that those responsible for the crimes were members of the state (the army, police or government security forces);
- And in 89 of the murders and 10 disappearances, the evidence pointed to paramilitary groups which operate as auxiliaries to the army and police.

In other words, while a crime committed by drug traffickers which claimed 20 lives was widely reported by the international news media, 130 victims of state or para-state violence were ignored outside Colombia; they simply did not exist. Granted, these 130 cases occurred neither on a single day nor in a single place, and thus did not "fit" into the parameters of "international news." But the contrast between what is considered news and reported and what is not, helps explain the way false images are constructed.

Between May, 1989 and June, 1990, the period during which the most drug-related terrorist bombings were carried out, Colombian non-governmental organizations registered 227 drug-related fatalities. During the same period they registered 2,969 politically motivated murders, not counting deaths in combat between the army and guerrillas. Thus drug related murders were only 7.6% as high as those from political violence.

Indeed, between January 1991 and May 1992, drug related deaths represented only 0.18% of the total number of violent deaths occurring in the country.

This stereotype linking violence in the country to drugs that the international media have created has served the Colombian government well. On the one hand, it has enabled it to present itself in international forums as a "victim" of violence outside its control by drug traffickers and the guerrillas, and, on the other, permitted it to neatly conceal crimes of the state which exceed these others many times over but which are so rarely mentioned in the international media.

Between 1988 and 1992, the Colombian armed conflict between the army and guerrilla claimed a total of 6,040 victims, including soldiers, guerrillas and civilians caught in the cross-fire. This figure represents 4.7% of the country's total violent deaths and 30.5% of the politically motivated killings during the same 5 year period. 70% of these latter killings must be explained in some other manner.

2. Counting the Victims: A Painful and Controversial Task

In August, 1986, during its annual assembly, the Conference of Religious Superiors of Colombia approved the following resolution: "To promote, support and encourage the Christian prophetic signs which are present in religious communities, through the creation of a Commission of Justice and Peace which will channel and disseminate information and protests throughout the country."

The board of directors of the Colombian Catholic Conference of Bishops, however, did not approve of this initiative and placed obstacles in its path. Nevertheless, two years later a group of 25 Catholic provincials decided to found the Intercongregational Commission of Justice and Peace, subsequently adopted by the Conference as one of its official commissions. The Commission's first project was to gather and disseminate information about the victims of human rights violations, the right to life, in particular. To this end, we set up a data bank and began registering such cases.

Our first difficulty involved agreeing on categories for the different kinds of violence that we were registering. Convinced as we were that the term "human rights," for historical, philosophical, legal, ethical, political and pragmatic reasons, refers essentially to the relations between citizens and the state, we attempted to classify cases according to the direct or indirect responsibility attributable to government agents. But this proved impossible.

Beginning in the early 1980s, Colombians began to be caught up in what we call a "Dirty War." A vast network of armed civilians began to replace, at least in part, soldiers and policemen who could be easily identified. They also started to employ methods that had been carefully designed to ensure secrecy and generate confusion. Because of this, witnesses and victims of crimes are unsure of the exact identity of the individual(s) responsible for committing them. This problem with identifying the perpetrators is often insurmountable.

At the same time, members of the army and police began to conceal their identities, frequently wearing civilian clothes and hoods, to drive unmarked cars and to take their victims to clandestine torture centers, all in order to forego legal formalities in arrests. What has frequently followed these abductions is intimidation or torture, enforced disappearances and murder. They complement these practices with death threats against family members, witnesses, lawyers and any other individuals likely to denounce their activities. Frequently, members of the state or of paramilitary groups pass themselves off as members of "guerrilla units" when they commit crimes, leaving cryptic communiques at or near the scene of the crime. When reporting such incidents, the media depend almost exclusively on official (government/armed forces) versions of what has happened. This, in turn, reproduces and consolidates the misinformation.

For these reasons, we chose categories which we felt would permit us to differentiate between different kinds of violence that existed in the context of a Dirty War. We began to consider the motives which could be inferred from different characteristics of the crimes: the political and social context of the region where the crime occurred, the characteristics of the victims, their participation in union activities, campesino, community or other kinds of political organizations, and their involvement in denunciations or other kinds of protest activities.

- Cases in which it is possible to infer a political motive (repression of ideological or political beliefs) are classified as political killings.
- Cases in which the available information is not conclusive but still suggestive of such motives are classified as presumed political killings.
- Many other cases are classified as obscure, signifying that there is doubt as to whether or not the crimes were committed by common criminals.

Given the size and geographic complexities of the country and the impossibility of maintaining systematic contact with many of its regions, we obtain initial information of violent deaths from the study of 17 regional and national newspapers, after first attempting to strip accounts of the frequent bias in which they are reported.

Soon, in spite of the repugnance its name caused us, an additional category had to be created: social cleansing killings, referring to the physical elimination of drug addicts, exconvicts, petty thieves and criminals, prostitutes, homosexuals, beggars and street children. Tragically, such killings are a routine practice today, part and parcel of the generalized expansion of violence in the country which began in the 1980s.

Although different interests are involved, indications from a large number of these cases point to members of the national police as being responsible. Anecdotes revealing how accepted this practice is within the police abound. "It's better to eliminate them because if they are arrested and tried, they'll just be freed in no time or there will be nothing to charge them with, and, in a couple of days, they'll be back again, a problem for the police. " Behind this abhorrent practice is a neo-Nazi ideology prevalent within the police which legitimates the taking of human lives.

Beginning in 1988, we began to circulate a quarterly bulletin containing a systematized analysis of the dimensions of the country's political violence. The statistics were, and continue to be, frightening. Consider the following, The Truth and Reconciliation Commission in Chile registered 2,700 cases of political murder and disappearances during 17 years of brutal military dictatorship in that country. This number of cases, horrible as it is, is far less than the number of cases our data bank has registered *annually* in each year since it began operation.

Indeed, a number of religious communities and orders were so horrified when they read the first issues of our bulletin that they sent us letters asking us to stop publishing lists of victims, saying they only depressed them. We didn't heed their request. We feel that there should be a historical record of what has happened and that the victims merit, at the very least, a brief mention documenting their fate as a testament to the failure of so many efforts to relegate them to oblivion and silence. In scores of cases, these few lines are the only written testament to their human dignity.

The Colombian government, for its part, has become more and more uncomfortable with our lists. As I was writing this in June of 1994, the Presidential Counselor for Human Rights invited me to participate in an Indicators Workshop "intended to discuss and share criteria for the elaboration of statistics about violence in general, political violence and human rights violations."

During the workshop's final session, and in front of delegates from all of the government's investigative organizations, the counselor lashed out at our interpretation of political violence. In particular, he objected to the fact that we categorized cases as presumed political killings, and argued that such a category blamed the government for cases where responsibility for the crimes was unclear.

He also criticized us for considering "social cleansing killings" to be the product of a neo-Nazi ideology which prevails within certain government institutions. He insisted, instead, that such practices were carried out by "isolated" individual agents; he was opposed to our registering paramilitary crimes as part of official violence, and so on.

In my talk I attempted to defend our position by insisting that we could not limit ourselves to simply registering cases in which responsibility had been established because the "Dirty War" strategy had, since the early 1980s, been refining and perfecting methods of secrecy, concealment and impunity for those responsible. To register only cases in which the responsibilty was clear would grossly distort the dimensions of what is really going on in the country.

3. Scenes from the "Dirty War"

It is difficult for people to really understand the reality in Colombia, so different from their own, unless it is translated into concrete individuals, places, dates and incidents they can identify with on a personal level. Perhaps that is why global analyses, even when they refer to dramatic human situations, tend to be distant and cold. For this reason, 1 have chosen the following cases—from among several thousand—to talk about. They are cases and individuals I have had close contact with either because I knew the victims personally or because I shared the pain of family members, friends and whole communities as they made protests and embarked on the search for a justice that was not to be.

Caquetá

Caquetá is a department in southern Colombia and a region where peasant farmers have pushed further and further into the Amazon jungle. During the 1970s, the department was the center of important agrarian struggles, and, toward the end of the decade, home to the nascent M19 guerrilla movement. In 1981, in order to combat the guerrillas the army set up an operative command post there (No. 12) which would later become the XII Brigade. Caquetá was also home to a female missionary community which spent over 10 years working alongside campesinos in an integrated community development program based on Christian principles.

I will never forget the first week I spent in Caquetá in April of 1982. The large number of denunciations of torture, disappearance and murder that we had been receiving prompted me to travel to the region. When I arrived at midday at the modest dwelling of several members of a religious community and asked them if I could set up a meeting with family members of some of the area's victims, one of them looked at me and smiled. "Just take a seat over there, Father. there are so many that come to tell us what has happened to them and how they have suffered...well, just sit down for a moment." She was right, I spent the next four full days taking notes and taping interviews, taking time out only to visit two nearby villages and talk to more victims. When I returned to Bogota, I took with me a macabre list of 144 murder victims, some of them had been subjected to extreme cruelty, and 240 cases of torture. In those days, there was no doubt as to who was responsible for these atrocities; soldiers killed and tortured openly in front of numerous witnesses. But it was impossible to identify them because, before committing crimes, they removed the identification they were required to wear by law.

Among those hundreds of cases, here are a few that stand out.

• A young woman, with a confused and almost hopeless air about her, answered my questions and spoke into my taperecorder. She had been forced to join a military patrol and walk for 13 days through the mountains, guiding the soldiers and carrying their knapsacks. Although she witnessed numerous cases of torture and the destruction and burning of humble campesino dwellings, it was the brutal murder of Jesús Pastrana which affected her the most. I myself had met this campesino leader on one of his visits to Bogota to attend meetings of the ANUC (a national peasants organization with strong support during this period). According to the terrible details the young woman gave me, Chucho, as Jesús was affectionately called, died a slow and agonizing death on October 31, 1981. He was hung from a tree as psychopathic soldiers cut off his ears, his fingers, hands, then arms and testicles and finally shot him 21 times.

• I was deeply moved as I listened to Florentino, a young campesino who had miraculously escaped from his own grave. At 9 p.m. on December 6, 1981, a group of soldiers dragged Florentino and his elderly father from their home, tied their hands together and gagged them and took them to a nearby military base where they were holding four other campesinos. At midnight, the men were taken into the mountains and forced to lie face down before an open grave that had been dug for them. Then, using knives and rifles, the soldiers began to kill them. Although seriously wounded in the neck, Florentino managed to feign death. One by one the bodies were thrown into the grave and each was covered up with dirt shoveled in by the soldiers. Suddenly, the killers were momentarily distracted by shouts from other soldiers standing beside a nearby river. Florentino took advantage of their distraction, and, after reaching out to his father's now cold body and realizing he was dead, fled into the nearby forest alone. Although the soldiers soon realized that "one of the dead men had escaped," they couldn't make him out among the trees in the darkness. Florentino made his way cautiously into the river and, swimming as best he could, finally reached a campesino's dwelling down the shore whose occupants helped stop his bleeding and assisted him in making his way to the city of Florencia (capital of the department).

• I will also never forget the sobs of the young catechism student as she told me of the martyrdom of Ernesto, a young member of a Christian base community. For having gone, or having been forced to go to a M-19 meeting of the guerrillas, Ernesto and a number of other young residents of his village, San Jose del Fragua, were tortured for 5 days on a military base. After the torture, Ernesto was freed on the condition that he report back to the army once a week. On these occasions, the base commander told him he had three alternatives: he could join the guerrilla in which case the army would sooner or later kill him; he could join a counterinsurgency unit and work as an auxiliary to the army; or, lastly, the commander told him, the army would not be responsible for his life and what might befall him. Although his friends insisted he flee the area, Ernesto's mother and family were financially dependent on him and he decided not to abandon them. He categorically refused to join the army, however, saying that would make him nothing more than a murderer, using the words that are so very common among our campesinos: "I don't want to do any harm to anyone."

March 25, 1982 was one of the days that Ernesto had to report to the army base, but that day he was afraid to go. Before he left, he told his mother, "Bless me, Mother, I think they are going to kill me." He was right. Members of the counterinsurgency group were waiting for him outside his house and that same day Ernesto disappeared. His body, showing signs of more torture, was found five days later.

Alvaro Ulcué Chocué

Alvaro was an Indian priest. When he was ordained in 1973, the ceremony made the national news because it was so very rare that an Indian entered the priesthood. A theology student at the time, I felt especially happy for him as I had always been particularly sympathetic to the struggles of the Indians of the Cauca department, heroic survivors of five centuries of oppression. I subsequently met Alvaro at different national meetings of Christian groups. Humble and soft-spoken, he was nevertheless totally committed to the liberation of his people. He took part in different Indian organizations, visiting the territories of other ethnic groups and was considered a leader by his people.

It was not long, however, before Alvaro's decision to work and struggle alongside his own people put him directly into conflict with the region's large landowners whose interests were in opposition to those of the Indians. After he suggested that his Indian parishioners stop choosing wealthy white people as godparents for their children, because landowners subsequently felt they had the right to demand their godchildren work for free on their haciendas, Alvaro became the target of the landowners. The army, too, had him in its sights, accusing him of leading Indian protests and marches in the region and inciting Indians to kill landowners.

By 1981, Alvaro was in the center of the storm. Landowners continued reporting him to the army, and even to the Archbishop, claiming he was inciting the Indians to violence. Soldiers continued abusing the Indians in order to provoke them, and, when they responded by protesting, increased their harassment. During one of these "incidents," Alvaro's sister Gloria was killed and his parents were injured after members of an army patrol attacked them as they were returning from a communal work project.

A communique made public in late 1982 by Christian groups in Cauca announced that "Landowners have placed a bounty on Alvaro's head and only the love shown by those who surround him has so far prevented him from being "disappeared."

Two days before he was murdered, Alvaro met with

three army generals to denounce the constant abuses the Indians were suffering and insist the army present evidence to back up their accusations against him. After listening to him in silence, the generals told him they were as convinced as ever that he was provoking the Indians into illegally occupying lands they had no right to.

On November 10, 1984, as he was preparing to officiate a baptism in the small town of Santander de Quilichao, Alvaro was shot and killed by two sicarios dressed in civilian clothes.

A witness who later identified both killers as members of the F-2, the intelligence service of the police, was subsequently harassed and received death threats. Soon after that, the case file of the investigation "disappeared" from the prosecutor's office. A mourner at Alvaro's funeral painstakingly copied the dozens of messages that mourners had written on placards and banners. One of these, echoing a thought he expressed on numerous occasions, said, "If I must die, I would like my body to be mixed in with the clay of the forts like a living mortar, spread by God between the stones of the new city."

Nevardo

When I think of Alvaro Ulcué, I cannot help but remember another young man in whom he inspired a commitment to the poor and the Indians and an individual, also like Alvaro, who paid the ultimate price for that commitment.

Nevardo was a restless youth. He wrote poems and songs and, although he wanted to become a Franciscan priest, the road was not easy for him. After spending two months with Alvaro Ulcué in Causa, Nevardo interrupted his university studies and went to work in some of the poor barrios in the city of Neiva, the capital of the

Huila department. There, he taught primary school and became involved, always with his songs and guitar, in different protests and struggles. It was really only after his death, by reading his diary and the many thoughts and notes he left in his notebooks and Bible, that it became clear how these different experiences had all been fragments of an intense personal search for the meaning of his life, in the light of the Gospel.

Luz Stella was one of the young people who participated with Nevardo in theater and Bible study groups, and, also like him, became more and more committed to the struggles of a nearby Indian community which, in spite of constant persecution and suffering, continued to struggle for a small parcel of land that had belonged to their ancestors.

They were confronted by a number of wealthy landowners who were armed with false land titles used to claim the Indians' land. The landowners, allied with the police, had so harassed and threatened members of the community that the Indians had been relegated to a small island in the Magdalena River. The island flooded with the advent of each rainy season. Arbitrary detentions and threats of Indians were soon followed by disappearances and murders.

The Indian Support committee, of which Nevardo and Luz Stella were a part, decided to begin work alongside a campesino community also struggling for land in another of the department's villages.

On October 22, 1987, Luz Stella and Nevardo, together with Carlos, the Indian community's governor, and Salvador, one of its members, set off to visit the community. As they were waiting for a bus in the town of Campoalegre, they were picked up by the local police. When members of a commission set up to look for them did so, police denied the party had been detained.

But they were found shortly thereafter. Three days later in Neiva, on a Sunday night, a thousand mourners joined the funeral procession for the four victims, whose decomposed bodies, horribly disfigured by torture, had been found earlier in the day.

All of the official investigations which were begun at our insistence proved fruitless. During a meeting in Bogota with the country's Prosecutor General, we offered to set up a support group and investigate the crime ourselves. Soon we had reconstructed the sequence of events, step by step, that led to the murders. Several months after our meeting, however, the Prosecutor General was assassinated. Several more months passed and the investigations were "closed."

I will never forget one of the young people who came to Bogota from Neiva to attend that first meeting in the Prosecutor General's office. His name was Aldemar and he had been one of Nevardo's closest friends. With little understanding of the legal arguments and complexities of the investigations, he was simply unwilling to leave things as they were and leave the meeting until he had at least been assured that something concrete would be done. Several years later, after Aldemar's mutilated body was found floating in the Cauca River near Cali, I was deeply moved as I read his diary and learned of the personal process of spiritual and political radicalization that had accelerated after his friend's death. Aldemar had been deeply touched by Nevardo's life and death. On April 15, 1992, Aldemar and five other leaders of popular, grass-roots organizations were "disappeared" in Cali. Several days later, their bodies, all showing signs of torture, were found.

I will also never forget that Sunday in October, 1991,

when at the urging of his mother, we tried to unearth Nevardo's remains. In spite of the fact that great pains had been taken to ensure that his grave would remain anonymous, six hours of digging a tunnel under another grave which had been placed on top of his finally led us to Nevardo. There, we saw for ourselves the cruelty that he had been subjected to: his skull had been completely destroyed and there were huge blood stains over what were left of his clothes.

Lucho

One day in 1989, in the city of Bucaramanga (capital of the department of Santander), a group of union members set up a meeting for me with a young campesino they had helped escape from the neighboring department of Cesar.

At first glance, the man seemed normal in appearance. He had a good sense of humor, and, if you spoke to him for only a short while, his tragedy remained hidden from you.

When you spent more time with Lucho, however, you learned of the continual nightmares which afflicted him and the screams that awoke the others who slept in the same room; of his dislocated knee and multitude of other health problems and his constant, agonizing headaches.

Lucho lived in a small town in Cesar, and, although not himself a union member, he had always worked as a farm day laborer. He was friends with several members and frequently spent time with them in their union hall after work. That presence alone was enough for the army to label him a "guerrilla auxiliary."

Lucho planned to go home early that November afternoon in 1988. He left the union hall with a friend but as they were passing a corner store, a group of laborers they knew called and invited them to have beer. The men drank quickly, both were in a hurry. But the group insisted they stay and have another. Suddenly and without warning, the men saw they were surrounded by soldiers. There was nothing coincidental about the men's presence there or the invitation; they had planned the encounter. There was no escape.

The men were forced into a house which stood opposite the corner store and belonged to a well-known politician and member of Congress. To their horror, they saw that the house also served as a training center for sicarios, a torture center and an army camp. First, their identification was taken from them; then, they were beaten and tortured until they lost consciousness. A soldier watching the torture told the men they would not be permitted to leave the house alive now that they had seen what really went on there.

Just before midnight, the two friends were told they would die crucified on crosses. Outside, men began to load huge trunks of wood and iron stakes onto a pickup truck that belonged to the politician. The men were then tied together and forced up into the truck. In whispered undertones they quickly agreed to try and escape at the first opportunity; being shot and killed was better than crucifixion.

It was after one in the morning when the truck began driving out of the town. Suddenly, a struggle began in the back, the driver turned to glance back at what was going on and the truck swerved sideways and hit the railing of a bridge. Both men jumped from the truck. One of the sicarios fired, killing Antonino immediately. But Lucho, vomiting blood, managed to get free from him, off the bridge and into the darkness. When lights began going on and people began looking out of nearby windows, the killers drove the truck back over Antonino's body and fled.

For Lucho, the ghost of his dead friend became a constant nightmare that never leaves him. More recently, another ghost, that of one of the sicarios who was subsequently murdered, has also begun to haunt him. The crowds of the big cities do nothing to dispel these ghosts; sometimes in the entrances to large stores he sees the dead, in the bodies of the living, pursuing him, as reality and fantasy mingle, confusing and hurting him. But it is not only the dead that pursue him; members of that group of soldiers and paramilitaries are also after him. His crime? Having been a candidate for the cross and having seen firsthand what was hidden behind the door of the congressman's house.

Alfonso

His voice broke when he told me that he had cried. Alfonso was a campesino, one of the "duros" or "strong ones" as we called them, a veteran of many struggles and he spoke from the heart. I think he cried not only for the friend he had saved but also for the solidarity of that campesino community and the creative spirit and force that had enabled it to snatch individuals from death's door. But even as he talked to me, Alfonso was aware that it was a solidarity that was being slowly beaten down and torn apart by the force of terror.

It happened in 1989. Almost everyone had given Alfonso up for dead. He had been taken away by an army patrol and his store, the rural hamlet's social meeting place, had been ransacked and destroyed. Several days earlier, soldiers had picked up a man with the same first and last name as Alfonso, torturing him for 12 hours before realizing their error. When they captured Alfonso, his death seemed a foregone conclusion, inexorably dictated by the laws of the "Dirty War."

All our initials attempts to rescue him led us to the same result; he was "disappeared." After the army denied any knowledge of his detention, our only option was to be alert for any unusual gathering of vultures, a sign of the presence of a body dumped somewhere in the countryside.

The community, however, was unwilling to simply give up on one of its own. Almost 100 of its residents set off for the city of Barrancabermeja. There, they entered and occupied the Prosecutor's office, demanding the country's Prosecutor General and other high-ranking government officials in Bogota be notified of what had occurred. Local authorities asked for assistance from the army's high command. Finally, the army agreed to release Alfonso and a group set off into the mountains to bring him back. After 10 days of torture, he was more dead than alive.

Some years later, Alfonso told me the details of the hell he had been through. Dragged out of his house with his hands and feet tied together, he was taken into the mountains and tortured, a shirt was forced into his mouth and down into his throat; he was beaten in the face until his teeth were broken, one of them pulled out with the roots; his eyes were burned with cigarettes; his nose was filled with salt water until he lost consciousness and he was beaten mercilessly about the neck, the abdomen and legs causing internal hemorrhages and the inflammation of a number of organs. This orgy of cruelty seemed imaginable only as a prelude to death.

His rescuers immediately took him to the hospital where he began medical treatment which would last for several months. In order to avoid further scandal, the mayor of Barrancabermeja agreed to cover all of his medical and hospital costs.

Although Alfonso's body and soul were permanently scarred by the horrible tortures he was subjected to, for him the terror continues. During the past few months (July/August 1994), both the army and the paramilitaries have begun to harass him again. I have gone with him to numerous meetings with government ministers, counselors and prosecutors, but we have been unable to obtain a genuine commitment from them to protect him. The region where he lives has been chosen as the center for one of the country's most terrible paramilitary projects. One consequence is that the terror has, in large measure, neutralized the solidarity of the community. As I write these very lines, l have received word that several of his neighbors are scrambling to abandon the region, looking for somewhere to go before it is too late.

A Lay Worker from Casanare

So pathetic was the story I heard from a lay worker who worked in the eastern department of Casanare, that I wanted to share it with you now.

It was such a very strange funeral procession, she said, with feelings of terror, indignation and impotence perhaps even stronger than the overriding sadness. A casual observer would be hard-pressed to distinguish between scenes of a war and scenes of a funeral; as the procession carrying the coffins of the two young people emerged from the church of that small village, soldiers took up positions on either side of them, machine-guns pointed and at the ready.

It had all started when the guerrillas entered the village and killed a soldier. Shortly afterwards, a contingent of 120 soldiers arrived and told the townspeople that at least 120 of them would die as a reprisal for his death.

In the days that followed, soldiers entered and searched most of the town's houses and, before long, almost all of its young people had been tortured. Then, one afternoon, the army gave the townspeople an order forbidding them from leaving their houses after 6 p.m.

The next evening, one of the two young victims hurried to a restaurant where he regularly ate supper. It was past 6, however, and he was captured by a group of soldiers.

Minutes later, his brother was startled by soldiers banging on the door of his house. Although his sister begged him not to go outside, he told her that he "had nothing to hide and, therefore, nothing to fear," and opened the door. The soldiers dragged him outside and took him away. The next day the brothers' bodies were found; they had been horribly tortured before being killed.

The decision was made to hold the wake in the school; after all, both boys were well-loved students. The townspeople would simply not give in to the terror that was inundating the town or to the soldiers who had arbitrarily labeled the two youths "criminals." Yes, even with the soldiers' guns pointed menacingly at them, the townspeople would celebrate their faith in human dignity and show that justice could not be destroyed in this manner.

And so the school's teachers and students, the parish and the townspeople honored the two young people. Under the circumstances, their act became an heroic one—and one which infuriated the soldiers who had orders to humiliate them and trample their rights, all in order to satisfy a perverse hunger for vengeance.

Nerves at the breaking point, fists clenched, words and screams bottled up in throats with no escape and tears like rivers of bitterness borne of pain, indignation and impotence, all combined to transform that silent funeral procession, amid the soldiers, the machine-guns and the fear, into an heroic tribute to life and human dignity.

San Vicente de Chucurí

It was February 21, 1990. A number of campesinos had arrived in Barrancabermeja after fleeing a rural zone near San Vincent de Chucurí that had been bombed by army helicopters and planes. I was in Barranca that day and, together with several members of the local Human Rights Committee, decided to go to the zone where, according to some of the campesinos, there were a number of wounded who needed medical attention and dead bodies which hadn't been identified.

The scenery as we traveled was breathtaking but then, as we made our way up the hill known as the Cerro de la Aurora, we began to notice pools of dried blood by the roadside, and craters that had been opened up by the bombs and rifle shells. The stories we were told by some of the campesinos who had stayed behind during the bombardment were chilling: the soldiers had grabbed one boy, they said, in the presence of many witnesses. Although the witnesses were subsequently forced into a farmhouse, all of them saw the army helicopter arrive and take the boy away.

The discovery a week later of a mound of fresh earth in a nearby hamlet alerted the campesinos. There, they found what was left of his body; it had been ripped into small pieces and they had to use two plastic bags to pick it up.

Near that same spot, two elderly deaf mutes, perhaps they didn't hear the bombs and for that reason didn't flee the area, were savagely tortured and murdered in their humble dwelling. When we entered we saw a puddle of wet blood amidst the disarray of their meager belongings.

One campesino woman in particular impressed me with her strength and acute powers of observation: "Father," she said, "I have lived in these mountains for fifty years and even from far away I know the difference between the smell of a dead animal and a human being." We went down with her about sixty meters, walking off and away from the path through a grove of trees. As we walked, the smell of death became more and more acute. As a few rays of the early afternoon sun filtered through the trees, we saw provisions scattered on the ground, evidence of a recently vacated army camp. Suddenly, we were confronted with a macabre spectacle, a man lay on the ground with his arms and hands extended and opened wide, his mutilated body looked as if it had been crucified. We stood silently, holding our breaths as emotions welled up within each one of us. I could think only of the "Requiem aeternam" and the verses from Job 19 that the Christian tradition has intoned over so many millions of coffins over the centuries, "I know that my Redeemer lives, and that in the end he will stand upon the earth. And after my skin has been destroyed, yet in my flesh I will see God, I myself will see him with my own eyes, I, and not another. How my heart yearns within me!"

The skin had been ripped away from his skull and it had several bullet holes in it, His hands, however, had enough skin on them to see that they had been burned in a bonfire; we found the ashes nearby. Ropes were tied around his feet and we guessed he had been dragged to this spot. The campesino woman who had guided us here pointed out something else, these were not the calloused hands and feet of a campesino, she said. She was right. That same night an investigative commission from the Prosecutor's office arrived, and, after taking skin samples from his fingers in order to identify him, ordered him buried.

Two years later, I learned that the man's identity had been positively established, Juan Fernando Porras, a doctor who had been "disappeared" by members of the B-2 (the army's intelligence unit) several days earlier in Bucaramanga.

He had been accused of collaborating with the guerrillas. Witnesses who were being held at the same cells of the army's Fifth Brigade later told of having seen him there under heavy guard.

The Campesino Hostel

The Middle Magdalena region is the valley carved out in parts of five departments by the Magdalena River as it winds its way northwards towards the Caribbean. Rich in minerals and fertile agricultural land, the Magdalena Medio is also a region where many different types of violence have taken root: guerrilla organizations have been based in the nearby mountains since the 1960s; the army chose the region to implement many of its most brutal counterinsurgency methods and refine its "Dirty War" strategy; and the paramilitary strategy which emerged in the 1980s has established strongholds in the region. The city of Barrancabermeja (known locally as "Barranca") is at the heart of the region.

In September, 1988, I was invited to participate in a human rights forum in Barranca. As we finished our expositions and discussions, a group of families arrived to denounce their displacement from the countryside around the neighboring municipality of Simacota forced by army bombardment. They asked us for help in "taking refuge" in Barranca.

Several months earlier, I had visited a campesino shelter near San Salvador and had thought then how urgently Colombia needed a similar kind of temporary shelter. The homeless families now before us became the impetus for us to take up the challenge. It was a challenge, however, which proved no easy task For a number of popular organizations, the church and many campesinos the first reaction when faced with such a proposal was fear. "But wouldn't such a place be a perfect target for more repression," they said. With little alternative, we had to give it a try, history would give us the only definitive answer.

All our attempts to obtain public land on loan from the government were in vain. With help through international solidarity groups, however, we were able to purchase an abandoned warehouse. In April, 1989, the Campesino Hostel was opened.

During its first two months of operation, hostel residents were the targets of threats and telephone terrorism. Guard shifts had to be organized to watch the hostel at night in case of sudden attack.

Once again, it was as a result of international pressure and a letter-writing campaign in which the "aliases" of many of the individuals responsible for the threats (identified as members of the B-2 army intelligence units) were mentioned, that the Hostel was able to begin functioning again in relative calm.

In mid-1991, however, the attacks began again in earnest. (In two successive nights in June, 1991, the hostel's walls were the target of machine-gun bursts; in October, 1991, two massacres were carried out just outside the hostel's front door, and, although residents themselves were not among the victims, subsequent telephone calls told them that, "you may have escaped this time, but next time you won't be so lucky." In March, 1992, a group of armed men forced its way into the hostel at 9 p.m. one night and threatened terrified residents at gun point for three hours. In May, 1992, a young woman who had visited the hostel on numerous occasions admitted to having been sent there by a paramilitary organization which operated under the coordination of the army's XIV Brigade. She said that she had been blackmailed into working for the group and that it was planning another attack on the hostel. Two days later, her disfigured body was found on a road leading out of Barranca.

We decided to temporarily close the hostel during April and May, 1993, and pressure the authorities to investigate these attacks. Lengthy meetings with officials from the offices of the Prosecutor General, the Presidential Counselor for Human Rights and the Attorney General, however, only confirmed my suspicions: at the very heart of impunity and the almost impenetrable mechanisms which have been designed to maintain it, is a total lack of political will to combat paramilitarism and stop the "Dirty War."

Finally, in April, 1993, the Colombian Attorney General invited me to a "dialogue" in his office with the Minister of Defense, intended to discuss the situation and reach some kind of informal agreement about the hostel. In spite of the voluminous evidence that already existed to the contrary, the minister vehemently denied the armed forces had anything whatsoever to do with the hostilities and attacks, agreeing only to send a "directive" to the region's army and police authorities asking them to respect the hostel. This half-hearted commitment and the pressure of numerous displaced campesino families with no place else to go, prompted us to reopen the hostel. On the night of March 21, 1994, however, members of an army patrol attempted to force their way into the hostel, firing once through the window. And, once again it was the international community which expressed itself in strong criticisms to the government and permitted the hostel to enter another period of relative normality, in spite of the reigning impunity.

To talk to any of the hundreds of people who have passed through the hostel is to come face to face with profound human tragedies. And it is to begin to understand different realities which are bound together by the terrible nature of crimes, enforced displacements and disappearances, bombardments and paramilitarism, all of them existing within the framework of impunity.

El Carmen de Chucurí

One morning in October, 1990, a group of people from another municipality in the Magdalena Medio, El Carmen de Chucurí, arrived at our offices in Justice and Peace. Among them was Father Bernardo Marín, El Carmen's parish priest and the municipal ombudsman. Both had escaped an attempt on their lives and feared they would never be able to return to El Carmen.

Although we had received a number of protests about a particular kind of paramilitary project that was being implemented in the El Carmen region, it was when I accompanied these two survivors on the rounds of different government and justice offices as they made their stories clear that I began to understand the real nature and dimensions of this criminal structure.

Since its founding in the early 1960s, the National Liberation Army, or ELN as it is called, has exercised a certain influence in and around El Carmen. The guerrilla priest Camilo Torres was killed in combat nearby in 1966. In the years since then, a considerable number of campesinos have at one time or another come to "sympathize" with the guerrillas. Others who have not at least become accustomed to living with their presence, and this situation has enabled the guerrillas to impose their decisions, on occasion, in the region. To the army, El Carmen is a region that has to be subjugated at all costs, and, to this end, it has designed a cure much worse than the disease, a strategy which entails forcing the region's residents to participate in counterinsurgency operations, killing those who refuse to take part.

A training center for sicarios which had been set up by the army in a nearby village in 1981 was chosen as the headquarters for this paramilitary project. As the project advanced through the countryside, rural communities were told they had three options: join the paramilitaries, leave the region or die.

It soon became clear that the paramilitary project enjoyed support in the highest echelons of government. Paramilitary bases were constructed next to military bases, meetings with campesinos were called by soldiers and run by paramilitaires or vice versa, census data and lists of campesino families and properly owners elaborated by the army turned up in the possession of the paramilitaries, and individuals detained by soldiers were turned over to the paramilitaries.

Residents were obliged to pay special "taxes" to support what became known as "la autodefensa," to purchase arms and take part in paramilitary patrols, even to turn over their young children for several months at a time for training and patrols.

Our Commission began to systematize protests we heard from El Carmen and we published two lengthy reports on the criminal project being implemented there. According to the figures we compiled, since 1987 more than 300 people who refused to join the paramilitaries or leave the region were murdered. Dozens of other atrocities, tortures, disappearances, extortion, rape and the destruction of houses and crops, with dates, places and exact circumstances were also documented. Several thousand people fled the region and today live in poverty, struggling to eke out a living in different regions of the country.

Father Marín, who had set up a network of base communities in rural hamlets around El Carmen, saw first hand what was being planned for his parishioners, and, for that reason, courageously insisted they resist the paramilitary advance. In a 1987 meeting in the hamlet of Islanda, paramilitary group members and soldiers concluded that one of the first steps that had to be taken in order to take over El Carmen was to get rid of Father Marín and a number of other influential individuals. They decided to kill them. On October 4, 1990, the army base commander in El Carmen ordered the police chief to confine all of his agents to barracks at nightfall. Two sicarios had spent 20 days readying their plan and that night they would kill the priest. The police commander, however, decided to listen to his conscience and disobey the army order, and, with several of his agents, went to the site of the planned murder to warn the priest. It was a warning that saved his life. Later that same week, the police commander was "transferred" out of El Carmen to another region of the country. Before he left, however, he urged Father Marín and several of the other probable victims to flee the region, saying they would now have no one to protect them. Grateful to him, they took his advice.

Our repeated protests did finally reach a number of high-ranking government officials, however, and on March 29, 1992, after compiling a thick dossier, they ordered the arrest of El Carmen's principal civilian paramilitary leaders. When a flotilla of helicopters arrived in El Carmen to take the men into custody, however, the army and paramilitaries provoked a riot in the town and the judges and other judicial employees who had arrived to arrest the men were forced to flee for their lives, empty handed. This aborted judicial mission resulted in a scandal that soon catapulted El Carmen into national news. The quest for "justice" had gone "too far" this time, it seemed, and would have to be neutralized.

Almost immediately the mass media began their attacks, falling in step behind the army and accusing anyone who denounced the situation in El Carmen as a "guerrilla collaborator." We were victims of this intense campaign for more than six months. The army, meanwhile, unable to eliminate Father Marin physically, decided to destroy him morally by framing him using the testimony of "secret witnesses" who went so far as to accuse him of "having taken boxes of ammunition to the guerrillas." The "faceless system of justice" that has been set up in Colombia during the past several years, in which secret witnesses, secret judges, evidence and testimony and "accusations" made and paid for with large amounts of money are all integral parts, is an excellent vehicle for these types of legal setups, especially when the army itself has been granted wide-ranging powers to manipulate evidence.

Daniel

Daniel was in the paramilitary. Born into a poor family in the department of Valle, he did his eighteen-month mandatory military service in the San Mateo battalion in the city of Pereira. He then accepted a job with the army as an "informant," working much of the time as a driver. Coincidentally, his brother Rubiel had been murdered while working at a similar job.

In March, 1990, Daniel was given intelligence assignments in the rural zone around the municipality of Trujillo. There, he traced the movements of a guerrilla group and identified several houses the guerrillas entered, passing the information on to an army major who was in charge of counterinsurgency operations.

Between March 31 and April 1, 1990, in what became known as the Trujillo massacre, Daniel was stunned to see the use the army made of his periodic reports. Just before midnight on the 31st, a combined army/paramilitary group dragged a large number of campesinos out of their houses, took them to the hacienda of a well-known drug trafficker and brutally tortured them, dismembering them with a chainsaw. The army major reserved the most brutal of the tortures for himself. The last assignment Daniel carried out for the army was to transport their headless torsos to the Cauca River and dump them into the water. As he witnessed these atrocities, Daniel overheard the name of one of the group's next victims, Father Tiberio Fernandez, Trujillo's parish priest. Then he escaped.

Almost a year later in a conversation, Daniel told me that that particular incident had left him confused. Until then, he said, he had been convinced that to fight the guerrillas was to serve his country. But after what he had seen, he began to ask himself: "Who are the bad ones and who is the enemy now?"

After the DAS (a government civilian security organization) refused to protect him any longer, this confusion prompted Daniel to seek refuge in the camp of a guerrilla group in the process of demobilizing its members. He subsequently gave detailed testimony of the horrors he had seen to officials from the Prosecutor General's office and a number of judges; on May 5, 1991, during an ill-advised visit back to Trujillo to visit his father, he was "disappeared."

I will not describe the incidents Daniel witnessed and related in a coherent and detailed manner to national and international investigative and humanitarian organizations because their cruelty is enough to wound anyone's human sensibility. I can only say that the tortures that were carried out in that farmhouse were rooted in some of the worst barbarism in the annals of history.

Father Tiberio Fernandez, the clergyman Daniel had overhead being discussed, was one of the victims of this unspeakable cruelty; his horribly mutilated body was found floating in the Cauca River on April 24, 1990. Tiberio was born into a campesino family, and, in his youth, became an agrarian leader and one of the first students at the Universidad Campesina, founded by the Jesuits in the city of Buga. Tiberio's enthusiasm for cooperative work flourished during his school days, and, when he was named parish priest of Trujillo, he began to organize what would in the next four years become a network of 20 small-scale, community enterprises. Tragically, many individuals who worked in these small enterprises were tortured and murdered along with Tiberio; to the army and the drug traffickers, these and most other popular, grass-roots organizations are only "fronts for the guerrillas."

When the individuals responsible for the Trujillo massacre were absolved by the Colombian justice system, we decided to take the case, on behalf of the 63 victims we were able to identify, to the Inter-American Commission of Human Rights of the Organization of American States. After two years official, government replies and proposals and counter-proposals from us, a September, 1994, meeting was set up in Washington and a proposal to seek an "amicable settlement," as permitted by the IACHR's statutes, was considered. The Colombian government proposed the creation of an extra judicial commission in order to reexamine the case files and evidence and generate recommendations. The fact that a broad-based commission of this nature, which included both government and nongovernmental representatives, would come into direct contact with the barbaric events of Trujillo, seemed to us a positive step, and, after insisting on several conditions, we accepted the proposal.

The Commission finished its work in January, 1995, concluding that the Colombian government was responsible, both for the crimes committed by members of the Colombian army and police as well as for the deliberate suppression of the truth and corruption of Colombian judicial employees.

After receiving the Commission's final report on January 31, the president of Colombia, in an unprecedented action, accepted responsibility on behalf of the government and announced plans to compensate a number of the victims' families. There were no determinations made, however, about how to punish those the Commission concluded were involved in the massacre. They had already been absolved by the country's justice system, the absolute impunity which continues is as blatant a challenge as ever to justice. The only possible solution, a trial by members of an international tribunal, is a possibility the Colombian government refuses even to consider.

The Putumayo

Putumayo is another of Colombia's southern departments bordering on Ecuador, a zone of colonization where peasants and their small settlements continue to encroach on the dense jungle that surrounds it. In 1990, a number of parish priests insisted I visit the region in order to collect evidence of atrocities they feared were being relegated to oblivion. After several visits, I was completely frustrated; people were terrified and no one dared speak out. "Anyone who opens his mouth here is a dead man," was the way the campesinos expressed it.

But by Easter week, 1991, in the words of one of the local priests, it seemed that "things were about to explode." He was right. A huge procession through the town's streets on Easter Wednesday seemed to confirm the fact that the townspeople were no longer willing to look the other way and turn their backs on the blood bath which was taking place around them.

Members of the anti-narcotics police, operating from a base they had in the town, and a large group of paramilitaries had implemented some of the "Dirty War's" most ruthless tactics in the region; to be between 15 and 30 years of age was synonymous with being a guerrilla and, therefore, a legitimate target of disappearance and murder.

In a Registry of the Deceased in one of the area's parishes, I found a list of 280 individuals who had been shot and killed in the preceding 5 years. Seventy percent of them were less than 30 years of age. I was told later that for every one of these registered deaths, there were at least 10 others that had gone unreported, simply buried quietly and secretly.

That Good Friday under a scorching sun, what seemed like the whole town's population walked slowly through the streets and the Stations of the Cross. I waited for a campesino who, taking advantage of an absence of military patrols along the water, had promised to pick me up on his motorcycle and take me along the river's shore.

After we got into a canoe and started upstream, the campesino pointed out the places along the shore where bodies were regularly discovered, many of them buried right where they were found. If a cross had been erected at each grave, there would have been no room left between the river's shore and the beginning of the jungle. So many people dead and buried, I cannot put into words the feelings that overcame me on that slow passage along the river's shore beneath the midday sun that Good Friday.

Further upstream a campesino on shore told us what he saw at night as he looked toward the river from his small dwelling: at about midnight, he said, a white car would drive up, open its doors and men would be forced out. The men were then shot in the forehead, their stomachs were cut open and filled with heavy stones and they were dumped in the river. In a hushed tone, the campesino told us where we could find one of the survivors of these nightly massacres.

Following his instructions, we headed into the undergrowth, walking until we reached the shack of the young man named Arturo who told us his story. He had been picked up and arrested as he was walking past the anti-narcotics base. He was shut into a cell; later, several other young men were brought in to join him there.

Hours later, at about midnight, as they were sleeping on the floor of the cell, the men were woken up and taken outside to a white car. They were driven to the river, pulled out one by one, shot and kicked down into the water. Arturo was terrified. Feigning absolute naivety, he begged the men not to throw him into the river as he said he couldn't swim. Perhaps intent on watching him struggle and drown before shooting him, the men were stunned as Arturo suddenly dove as deep as he could into the river and swam under water to the other shore. The men's shots came up short and, by remaining motionless in the darkness, Arturo managed to go unnoticed. The frame of a small boat anchored near him served as protection and he was able to lift his head out of the water from time to time to breathe without being seen by the men.

Getting Arturo out of the region and to the capital so that he could tell what had happened to him and try somehow to stop the blood bath was difficult and risky. The army set up checkpoints along the river, the roads and at the airport. Tragically, in spite of the details of Arturo's story, justice was never served.

The director of the national police "transferred" the agents and police officers out of the region. But isn't it likely that they are simply doing the same thing in another part of the country? And, today, all these crimes and the individuals who committed them remain unpunished.

Riofrío
    On October 5, 1993, nightly television newscasts led off with the story of a successful military operation

which had resulted in the deaths in combat of "13 guerrillas" in the El Bosque rural hamlet, a municipality of Riofrío department of Valle. The next day, the story was front page news in all of the country's major newspapers.

Several days later, we established direct contact with several of the survivors. A commission, including a delegate from the Catholic Church and several nongovernmental human rights organizations, traveled to the zone, visited the scene of the crime and interviewed a number of witnesses. Some of these had talked to members of official government investigative teams which visited the hamlet; others, however, chose not to, preferring to tell what they had seen, in strict confidence, to members of the NGO commission. The information this commission collected laid bare both the army's monstrous capacity to lie and the mass media's complicitous role in covering up such crimes.

In reality, the "13 guerrillas" were members of two campesino families who had dedicated many years to making El Bosque a progressive and united hamlet, fomenting a genuine community spirit among its inhabitants. But to the army, all this organization was only a sign of the hamlet's ties to the guerrillas. Once again, the doctrine of collective responsibility resulted in another horrendous crime: given the fact that members of a guerrilla group passed through El Bosque from time to time, the families they visited were "guilty" and thus had to be eliminated. In addition, a drug trafficker from the Cali drug cartel had El Bosque's land in his sights. He owned much of the surrounding land and wanted to eliminate any possible resistance to his plans of controlling the area.

Just before dawn on October 5, members of the

Ladino and Molina families, leaders of El Bosque, were awakened and dragged out of their houses by a group of armed men wearing army uniforms and civilian clothes. The victims were taken up a path to the unoccupied house of one of the Ladino sons who had left the day before on an errand. There, the massacre was carried out, preceded by tortures and rapes.

Several of the survivors, some of them hidden among the nearby coffee bushes and others (women and children) shut into their rooms by the killers, saw soldiers arrive to relieve the armed group at about mid-morning. Both groups were in the same place at the same time. About noon that same day of the massacre, the mother of the victims was visited by a number of army officers. When she raised her head to look at the soldiers, she recognized one of them as having been with the first group earlier in the morning.

Colonel Becerra, Commander of the army's Palace battalion in the nearby city of Buga, claimed full responsibility for the military operation. It had been a "combat," he said, with an "extremely dangerous guerrilla unit," preceded by careful "intelligence" work which had resulted in the "deaths" of 13 guerrillas. In spite of his repeated public claims of having participated directly in the events which led to the 13 deaths, claims that were subsequently supported by Commanders of the army's Brigades and Divisions in Cali, the Prosecutor General's office chose to accuse Becerra only of "covering up" a mysteriously armed group which arrived at dawn and carried out the massacre.

Colonel Becerra had a dark past. When he was accused of being responsible for the 1988 massacre of 20 banana plantation workers in the Urabá region and a warrant was issued for his arrest, his military superiors enrolled him in a "promotion" course for officers and sent him to the United States. On his return to Colombia, with the arrest warrant still outstanding, he was promoted from colonel to lieutenant Colonel by an Advisory Junta from the Ministry of Defense made up of 26 Generals.

When we solicited an explanation of these mockeries of justice from the Prosecutor General, he replied that the investigation for Becerra's participation in the banana workers massacre had been terminated on April 20, 1992, and that an investigation against the generals from the Advisory Junta who approved his promotion was in its "preliminary stage" (four and a half years after the fact and six months before it could be legally terminated).

4. The Internal Logic of Colombia's "Democra-tatorship"

The term "democra-tatorship" was coined by the Uruguayan writer Eduardo Galeano who was unable to find a word in the dictionary to adequately describe a political system which combines democratic formalities with features and characteristics of a dictatorship.

Colombia is frequently characterized as one of Latin America's "most stable democracies." During the past 50 years, it has been ruled only once, 1953-1957, by a military dictatorship and it was one of the few countries which escaped unscathed from the era of the "National Security dictatorships" which sprang up in so many other South American countries during the 1960s and 1970s. Levels of political violence in Colombia, however, are much greater than those in any of these other countries.

A brief look at several characteristics of the country's political history help explain the particularities of the Colombian model and show how it has been able to assimilate so completely the main principles of the Doctrine of National Security within the formalities of a democratic framework These elements can be described as follows:

1) A political arena which was divided into two compartmentalized spheres. First, there is the bureaucratic/administrative, where the country's political parties compete and bureaucratic and budgetary spoils serve as an incentive for cycles of generalized corruption. The second sphere is the country's social conflict, which was turned over to the armed forces for management. In order to facilitate this, legislation incorporated into the State of Siege equipped the armed forces with rights to carry out extensive repression. By definition, this is an exceptional and transitory state of affairs during which the president can legislate by decree and suspend individual and collective rights and guarantees. Its principal instrument is the "fuero militar" or military privilege which permits members of the armed forces and police guilty of crimes to be investigated and tried by their peers in military courts, courts in which impunity has been all but institutionalized.

2) It is difficult to imagine an internal guerrilla conflict existing for as long as Colombia's, more than 30 years, without the existence of some kind of social legitimation and support in the country. The development of eight guerrilla organizations during the past three decades in Colombia led to the notion of the country's "internal conflict" as being part and parcel of the hemispheric conflict between the super powers. The country's guerrillas were considered the "enemy within the country." Colombian President Turbay Ayala (1978-1982)

characterized the country's armed insurgency as "the national spearhead of the international advancement of communism." Since they were the enemy, it became "acceptable" to deny its members their fundamental rights.

The country's media played, and continue to play, an important role in this regard, legitimating and justifying the deaths of guerrillas that occur outside of combat by suggesting that guerrillas can be legitimately "disappeared" or tortured, for example, and maintaining that guerrillas have no recourse to even the most fundamental procedural rights. The media have been successful in this not by the logic of their reasoning or the strength of their argument, but rather by the use of more subliminal methods, by manipulating and distorting or simply failing to report "news" and by tacitly endorsing such criminal practices.

Once these practices were legitimated and accepted for "guerrillas," it was not difficult to extend them to guerrilla collaborators, a label that was imposed on virtually all expressions of the country's popular movement and political opposition. And it was even easier to attach this label to inhabitants of the country's so called "conflict zones"; in these areas, the doctrine of "collective responsibility" was implemented. Campesinos, indigenous people or individuals who simply live in areas where guerrillas are active are considered guerrilla supporters or, at the very least, responsible for their presence and, therefore, legitimate targets of counterinsurgency operations.

3) During the 1980s, however, two cracks developed in this model, the first, as a result of a growing public awareness of human rights and the second, as a result of the progressive collapse of "international communism,"

which would eventually pull most of the ideological framework out from under the Doctrine of National Security.

The first crisis was counteracted by the design and implementation of the paramilitary strategy. The government was able to successfully conceal its role in and evade responsibility for crimes by entrusting much of the "dirty work" to armed civilian groups which began to operate under the clandestine coordination of the army and police.

The support some paramilitaries subsequently received from one sector of the country's drug Mafia further confused the issue and enabled the authorities to attribute almost any crime to "unknown individuals," individuals who were always conveniently neutral, called "narcoterrorists."

In order to deal with the second crisis, the country's "internal enemies" were reclassified as "terrorists," with the term terrorism being defined so ambiguously in the Colombian criminal code that today it can be applied to almost any expression of political opposition, discontent or popular protest.

4) Both the paramilitary, "Dirty War" strategy and the strategy of criminalization (or "terrorization") of social protest in the country, however, are vulnerable and open to being challenged in the legal arena. For this reason, it was necessary to carry the conflict into the judicial system. To do this, the new Colombian constitution designed a highly politicized model of justice which permitted the Executive to exert an inordinate amount of influence on many of the judiciary's key appointments, and in particular the office of the Attorney General, in which enormous discretionary powers are concentrated. The constitution also permitted the establishment of a

parallel justice system for members of the country's political opposition, adopted as part of the country's "ordinary" justice system, which includes such abhorrent characteristics and procedures as secret judges, witnesses and evidence, paid "informants," arrests and imprisonment prior to the initiation of any investigation, the acceptance of "military intelligence reports" as legal evidence, the prolongation of jail terms without trial or the existence of any sustainable evidence, etc. Today, this combination of arbitrariness and impunity is one of the Colombian democra-tatorship model's most important elements.

5) And, finally, it is difficult to register so many killings year after year without giving the impression that the government shares at least part of the responsibility, if only for its indifference and inactivity.

Surely the international community cannot help but be concerned when Colombia has had the dubious honor of being the world's most violent country for the last decade. To counteract these worries and give the world the impression that it has gone to great lengths to protect human rights in the country, the government decided to take up the human rights "banner"in name at least, and incorporate it into its political agenda. The new constitution was crucial in this regard, entrenching almost all of the existing international human rights declarations (all of them signed and ratified on numerous occasions by Colombia) and creating a variety of official organizations to protect human rights. The government, for its part, followed the constitution by multiplying the number of official human rights committees and organizations.

Those of us who make almost daily rounds of these offices, however, experience firsthand the reality behind

the rhetoric and know only too well that while each ful-
fills its own limited function, in an endless sending and
receiving of documents and files, seals and official
papers, none of them has the power to actually solve any
concrete problem. What they do do, however, and
admirably so, is add the one final cosmetic touch to the
democra-tatorship model.

5. A Society without Alternatives?

Decades of suffering in many Latin American countries have left scars which are frequently difficult to per-
ceive. They are overlooked, perhaps, because of the
sheer number of reports and declarations that have to be
dealt with; because of the urgency of finding solutions to
particularly pressing problems; the desperate fight to
obtain small victories and the euphoria they bring when
obtained or, perhaps, the hope that leads us at times to
take refuge in unattainable utopias as a defense mechanism against so many frustrations. Today, a talk or an
article which examines the kinds of deplorable situations
I have touched on here, without somewhere suggesting
what can be done to overcome them or proposing a solution, is considered incomplete. But this kind of hope and
optimism has become a social necessity. Society, too, has
erected its own defense mechanisms against despera-
tion.

Before suggesting a solution, however, I want to
mention one additional point, the consequences that so
many years of tragedy and suffering have had on our
society.

The struggle to convince victims of human rights
abuses of the need to denounce the crimes they have
been subjected to in order that they themselves do not
become the promoters of impunity, is a scene that has

become commonplace in my office over the years.

Predominant in all cases is the instinct for self-preservation. Individuals who have been able to save themselves or their loved ones do not want to put their lives into any more danger by denouncing what has happened to them and demanding justice. And, of course, they have all the reason in the world to feel this way. But it is precisely this attitude that permits the abusers and the criminals to remain untouchable. Sometimes when we talk of the need to fight against impunity, they seem to awaken with the challenge and their eyes shine. And, yet, when it comes time to talk of practicalities and where we can start, just as suddenly it all disappears. In their eyes is a mixture of shame and skepticism, it is as if they are telling me: "I made it this far. Now, the best I can do is wish you luck."

It is very painful to witness the breakup of marriages because one or the other partner can no longer stand the terror and the fear that the path towards justice entails or because he or she sees there will be no future for the children who are so often caught in the middle.

I was deeply moved one morning in my office by the tears of a banana plantation worker, a man who had witnessed murder and torture and received death threats, and yet had had the courage to denounce what he saw. But he had to leave his job and his home and now he had been given an ultimatum: in order not to lose his wife and mother, he would have to cut off all links with any popular organization and distance himself forever from any grassroots struggle or protest. His family could simply not stand the fear and persecution any longer. He made the decision to cut off all links with any popular organization and distance himself forever from any grassroots struggle or protest, but it had cost him dearly.

Another incident which touched me deeply and left me with a number of unanswered questions comes to my mind often. While participating in a course with a number of workers in Barrancabermeja, a campesino took me aside. He wanted to tell me about a difficult decision he had made, it still worried him, he said, and he wanted to share his feelings with someone. He told me that the army had set up a checkpoint in the countryside where he lived. Each day they stopped the local farmers and searched them. When campesinos arrived with fruit or vegetables, the soldiers scattered them on the ground or simply destroyed them, accusing them of "taking food to the guerrillas." For several months, the campesinos secretly organized a march to nearby Barrancabermeja where they occupied a local church as a symbol of protest. The government sent a representative to meet the campesinos, and, sympathetic to their plight, were given a signed agreement which stated the government would not permit any further abusive treatment by the army. On their return, however, the campesinos were stopped at the same checkpoint, searched and abused as before. When they showed them the signed agreement, the soldiers laughed and told them: "Those guys might be in charge in Bogota, but we call the shots here."

The campesino told me that it was at that moment that he lost whatever faith he had had in the government and its institutions and decided to join the guerrillas. A lump in my throat stopped me from saying anything to him for a long while. Here was a man who had sacrificed a great deal because of a belief that nonviolent methods could be effective. And now his hopes had been irreparably dashed.

What alternative could I give him that he had not already considered and found worthless? When I tried to tell him that failures, suffering and discontent would also almost surely be part of his life as a guerrilla, he said he knew that, but that all he wanted to do was die with dignity. In any event, he said, they were going to kill him sooner or later. Since then, I have often asked myself how many other combatants have decided in similar fashion to join the guerrillas, embarking on a hopeless struggle because somewhere or somehow they find in it a kind of ultimate hope and meaning.

In this regard, I can recall a discussion with the mothers from the Plaza de Mayo in Buenos Aires. The contemporary political situation in Argentina would seem to be proof that those years of brutal dictatorship were successful, not only in exterminating one entire ideological generation, but also in effectively conditioning, through terror, the one that succeeded it. An implicit but irrevocable decision seems to have been made by the new generation: never again to tread the ideological paths of the "disappeared," the tortured and the murdered. It is a kind of subconscious compromise to their wish to live.

These same thoughts came to my mind one morning as I read the column of a well-known journalist in one of Colombia's large newspapers: "Why are we against having certain left- wing political movements participate in Parliament," he asked, "Aren't they only a "controllable" minority? What are 10 or 20 votes, after all, compared to more than 100 of the traditional parties? Doesn't this all enhance the Congress's image as a democratic, pluralistic institution which represents all of the country's opinions?" There would be cause for alarm, he concluded, but only if this minority grew.

The smugness of these assertions has its origins in a situation not unlike that of the mothers of the Plaza de Mayo. Democracy and respect for fundamental human rights has a price: do not seek alternatives to the existing system.

When Presidential Counselors in Colombia tell the media that there has been a notable improvement in the country's human rights situation, and point to a reduction in 100 or 200 cases among several thousand total victims, many of us ask ourselves what price has been paid for this. Aren't there perhaps fewer people to be killed today than there used to be? Fewer campesinos willing to join a protest march or fewer workers ready to join a union and go out on strike? Couldn't it be that there are simply fewer people willing to denounce crimes and demand justice?

I have mentioned these incidents and made these reflections in the hope that they shed some light on a dimension and consequence of repression that is frequently overlooked—the destruction of a society's moral conscience.

When fundamental ethical questions cannot be explored because social structures force the instinct for self-preservation to prevent that from happening, the moral conscience of that society is being destroyed at its deepest levels.

6. Impunity: The Key Element

Many sociologists maintain that there is no clear relation between poverty and violence and that widespread violation of economic rights does not ordinarily result in violence. Others insist that violent reactions are more likely to occur when there is a large and obvious gap between the rich and the poor.

Whatever the answer is to this dispute, there is a closer relationship between the violation of civil and political rights and violence. Limiting or denying certain sectors the possibility of political participation is more likely to result in the evolution of an armed insurgency.

Colombia is a case in point. Until the 1970s, the country's political arena was the exclusive territory of the Liberal and Conservative parties; alternative political forces were considered illegal, especially if they enjoyed authentic, popular support in which case they were violently persecuted by the government and the targets of campaigns to delegitimize and even "demonize" them. Perhaps this can help explain why eight guerrilla organizations (and several other small and more fleeting groups) have evolved in the country since the 1960s.

The 1991 constitution, however, was inspired by different philosophies. Although clearly falling within the liberal tradition, it is nevertheless scarred by a number of clearly anti-democratic features: the justice system, the "fuero militar"," the states of exception and a transitory article which permitted decrees passed under the State of Siege between 1984 and 1991 to be converted into permanent legislation, in particular.

Today, less and less of the Colombian "problem" is situated in problems with existing law. That wasn't always the case. I remember participating in the country's first human rights forums in the early and mid-1980s. In those days, our conclusions invariably called for the following: the abolition of the law which permitted civilians to be tried in military courts; the lifting of the State of Siege and a number of decrees which had been passed under it, such as the Security Statute of 1978; the derogation of the legal framework for the creation of paramilitary groups (Law 48/68); the appointment of civilians as Delegate Prosecutor for the Armed Forces and Defense Minister; the signing and ratification of certain international human rights agreements, etc.

Fifteen years later, all of these changes in the law have been achieved. But violence and human rights abuses continue unabated, a clear indication that the problem is centered in other areas.

The country's different "peace processes" or dialogues over the years between the government and the guerrillas have taught us a lot in this regard. During the Betancur administration (1982-1986), an Amnesty Law for guerrillas renouncing the armed struggle was passed (Law 35/82).

Almost immediately, however, it became clear just how risky a proposition it was to depend on this law for protection as scores of amnestied guerrillas were murdered, frequently only hours after legalizing their situation. The Patriotic Union (UP) political party, another fruit of the Betancur peace process, was founded in November, 1985. Since then, a UP party member or supporter has been murdered every 53 hours. In the party's first four years of existence, this persecution was even more intense with a murder every 39 hours, and, in the run-up to elections, even more chilling, one every 26 hours.

As I write these lines, I think of the funeral of the most recent UP senator, assassinated on August 9, 1994. The procession was not nearly as large as others; but then to many, being a member of the UP means living with a death sentence. In 1993, Colombia's Human Rights Ombudsman was asked by the country's Constitutional Court to report on the progress of criminal investigations into the murders of UP party activists.

Of the 717 cases he examined (only a third of the total number of victims, the others apparently did not merit an investigation), only 10 had resulted in a completed investigation and sentence, 6 of them were acquitted.

We frequently put our faith in the justice system as a possible way out of the crisis we are faced with. If it only worked, we think, maybe the criminals would stop acting so wantonly and openly.

Successive Colombian governments have promised to "strengthen the justice system" in order to solve the serious problems of violence and impunity. In this regard, the European Union and the government of the United States have contributed significant amounts of money to help "bolster" the justice system. And yet levels of impunity in the country remain scandalously high: in April, 1994, at the end of the Gaviria administration, the Director of National Planning revealed that only 21 of every 100 crimes in the country are reported to the authorities, and, of these, 14 result in an incomplete investigation, only 3 of them leading to a sentence. This leaves a rate of human rights abuse where 97 percent of the crimes go unpunished. According to a June, 1993 report on the human rights situation from the Prosecutor General's office, the organization responsible for investigating and sanctioning government employees, less than 10 percent of all the complaints received (and relatively few are ever filed) are investigated; of them, 21 percent result in some kind of ruling. Of those in which members of the armed forces are involved, 57 percent result in absolutory sentences.

Why doesn't the Colombian justice system work? Most people don't believe in the system precisely because they know it doesn't work (a vicious circle?), choosing, instead, to seek forms of private justice or simply resign themselves to impunity. In cases where crimes against humanity have been committed, it is extremely difficult to convince a victim, a family member or a witness to testify or become involved in the criminal proceedings. To do so, they are certain, would be to sign their own death warrant or result in persecution and a never-ending series of threats against them and their families. How is it possible to give them faith and strength when the list of individuals who have denounced abuses only to be murdered or disappeared continues to grow?

In spite of all this, however, there is a courageous minority who will not resign itself to injustice and chooses to denounce crimes. Even these rare cases, though, run hard up against the wall of impunity. When the evidence is solid and irrefutable, cases are transferred out of the ordinary justice system and into the military "justice" jurisdiction where members of the armed forces investigate and try each other. Here, the fusion of institutional (military) authority and judicial authority frequently means that the officer who gave the order to commit a crime finds himself presiding over the jury responsible for trying the soldiers who carried it out.

When cases don't "fit" into the military jurisdiction or are being investigated by the Prosecutor General's office, the Dirty War's methods and clandestine mechanisms, refined and perfected now for over a decade, see to it that they rarely make it out of the "limbo," technically known as "Preliminary Investigations." This term, in practice, has little or nothing to do with the verb "investigate." Indeed, unless the victim, his or her family members or a nongovernmental organization carry out the investigation themselves, collect the evidence and take it personally to government employees who rarely leave their offices, cases are almost always closed and filed away, after a "prudent" period of time has passed.

But what kind of evidence can victims and their families bring? Only a recounting or a testimony given by those who secretly witnessed the crime or what ensued afterwards and are not too terrified to say so. Such testimonies, however, have become less and less accepted by the government. Sometimes their credibility is arbitrarily discarded, as was the case in the murder of the Swiss layworker, Hildegard Feldmann, (September 9, 1990) in which investigators from the Prosecutor General's office rejected 24 coincident testimonies, taken by different individuals on different days and in different places. Instead, the Prosecutor General's office chose to accept the version of 4 soldiers; 3 of them had participated in the murder and the other had not even witnessed it. This decision was based on the absurd argument that "the interests of the offended party might result in a distortion of the truth."

On other occasions, attempts are made to invalidate such testimonies by using other contradictory ones. This was the case in El Carmen de Chucurí; the investigators did not bother to check the veracity of events and incidents alluded to in the original testimonies. In this instance, they could easily have double-checked the more than 300 names which appear in the parish's registry of the deceased, for example. But they didn't bother. And, of course, the country's "secret justice system" is well set up to buy just these kinds of contradictory "testimonies." (These purchases are in addition to the others it buys in order to falsely accuse of being terrorists or guerrillas individuals who denounce crimes or clamor for justice, such as Father Marín, El Carmen's parish priest).

What, then, can be done? Here, I cannot emphasize enough the importance of impunity in this whole scheme of things—it is the principal key both to the democra-tatorship model itself as well as to the disastrous consequences it has had on society. Impunity

- leaves structures intact and gives implicit assent to the behaviors which enable crimes to be committed, clearing the way for them to continue;
- legitimates conduct to society which radically destroys civilized human coexistence;
- breaks the laws which have been established against such crimes and thus renders them invalid in practice;
- destroys trust in the country's justice system and leaves its citizens unprotected in the face of crime;
- encourages the search for forms of private justice and the development of multiple forms of violence;
- constitutes an additional affront to victims, their families and all those who are touched morally by the effects of such crimes;
- erodes the credibility of the country's institutions, in particular, those most involved in the perpetration, complicity and tolerance of crimes;
- destroys the fundamental basis of legitimacy of the State of Law;
- creates an atmosphere of the fatalistic acceptance of Crimes of the State in society which results in the exercise of certain civil, political and social rights being considered highly risky practices, rendering them inoperative in practice;
- and finally, it conditions and determines social behavior and ideological positions with a subliminal censorship of any demands for justice or any position in favor of an alternative society.

Impunity hides behind the failings and inefficiencies of the justice system; the calculated "silence" and indifference of government institutions; the complicity of the "information" media; the sentimental manipulation of public opinion and the intimidation and threats of criminals.

Some arguments used to legitimate impunity, and absolve members of the army, police and government security forces who are responsible for crimes, fail to withstand even the most basic ethical analysis. For example, one line of reasoning posits the necessity of fighting crime with crime. There is the notion that equates amnesties and pardons designed for members of insurgent groups with those for members of the State who are guilty of crimes against humanity, suggesting they be granted the absurd "right to pardon themselves."

Religious justifications, making use of an illegitimate recourse to the Christian principle of reconciliation which denaturalizes the Christian value of forgiveness, have also been used. But the context of forgiveness is interpersonal relations—where its true Christian nature is realized, as a risk, laden, creative, a free and spontaneous act which seeks to overcome situations at the point of rupture by way of an act of faith in the oppressor which "remakes" him as a brother. There is no transparent translation of this concept of forgiveness to the judicial/political arena in which human relations are mediated by structures that elude the very dimensions that nurture forgiveness, gratitude, creativity and freedom.

The notion of "forgive and forget" is espoused today by Episcopal conferences in a number of different countries. But it completely overlooks the legacy that Christian theological tradition left in religious teachings.

This legacy attempted to extend the Christian value of forgiveness to the "masses," and, to that end, formulated its 5 classic conditions of authenticity, examination of conscience, repentance, intention to make amends, confession and atonement for harm or injuries.

A similar effort must be made in order to translate the value of Christian reconciliation to the judicial/political arena. There must be a public clarification and admission of guilt, an explicit condemnation of the mechanisms, structures and doctrines which facilitate crimes, the implementation of corrective measures to stop them from being repeated and reparation to victims and society. These must all be dealt with head-on and unequivocally. The very nature of a political community makes this imperative: unless there is an explicit and profound social sanction of crimes, internalized by society's members and engraved in society's "collective memory," such crimes are not truly delegitimated.

Without these conditions, the Christian value of forgiveness becomes a perverse expression of its real essence: from a fraternal and creative act to an act which covers up the institutionalization of crime and destroys the barriers which protect human dignity.

7. An Urgent Appeal

Colombian non-governmental human rights organizations believe that the struggle against impunity is crucial in order to stop the systematic violation of fundamental human rights in the country, and that it is a struggle in which the international community, through its solidarity and intervention, has an important role to play.

The campaign, "Colombia, Human Rights Now," which was begun in mid-1994, includes the following six points:

1) To lobby for the inclusion of Colombia in agenda point 12 of the United Nations Commission on Human Rights which deals with "the question of human rights violations in any part of the world" and for the appointment of a special United Nations rapporteur to Colombia, to supervise the country's human rights situation.

2) To combat and dismantle paramilitary groups and death squads.

3) To restrict the "fuero militar" (military privilege) to military crimes, excluding acts which violate human rights; create an independent commission to investigate clarify considered human rights abuses; trial and punishment for the authors of such abuses and justice and compensation for their victims.

4) To abolish the regional jurisdiction (secret judges) and implement a reform of the country's judicial system which will ensure the independence of judges and guarantee the rights of all parties.

5) To guarantee the security of displaced individuals for a voluntary return to the regions they were forced to flee, restitution of their land and compensation for damages suffered.

6) To achieve an agreement between the two parties in conflict in order to humanize and seek a negotiated solution to the country's internal armed conflict.

I thus appeal to Colombian solidarity groups outside the country to request that their countries" governments, ministers of foreign affairs and ambassadors at the United Nations vote in favor of the appointment of a rapporteur for Colombia and that they demand the Colombian government set up an independent commission to investigate and clarify crimes against humanity, with the participation of international organizations.

At the same time, through letter writing campaigns, visits to Colombian embassies in different countries, etc., you can help us by insisting that measures are implemented in Colombia in order to:

- dismantle paramilitary groups;
- abolish the "fuero militar" for common crimes and, in particular, for Crimes against Humanity;
- abolish the "Faceless Justice System";
- guarantee a safe return and compensation for the displaced;
- achieve a political solution to the country's armed conflict.

Crimes against humanity are not characterized as such because they violate a given national or international legal order, but because they wound and offend the moral conscience of the human family. Questions of national sovereignty, consequently, cannot be used to impede the intervention of individuals or organizations of any nationality, race, language or condition in the defense of life and human dignity or in order to denounce and morally sanction what should never have occurred, in order that it never occurs again.

Paramilitarism
A Criminal Policy of the State
Which Devours the Country

To understand paramilitarism and how it functions in Colombia, it is useful to look at the root meanings of the term. Crisostomo Eseverri Hualde, the author of an erudite *Dictionary of Etymology of Spanish Helenisms*, published in Spain in 1944, notes the significance of the Greek preposition "para," used as a prefix in numerous Spanish language words. According to him, there are three meanings of this preposition: 1) approximation; 2) transposition; and 3) deviation or irregularity. In effect, this preposition is utilized to make reference to something which is next to, adjoining, which is similar to, but which at the same time is beyond, outside of, leaving from the entity denoted by the principal body of the word.

Some examples illustrate better the meaning: "parabiosis" denotes the union between two twin beings of which only one has its own independent life, while the other, a parabiotical, only lives at the cost of the first. "Paracite" (with a "c") is an abnormal cellular element of an organism; and a "parasite" (with an "s") is a living organism which feeds upon the juice of the other. The concepts of proximity and deformation are integrated, thus, in the meaning of this preposition.

According to the above, "paramilitarism" denotes activities close to military, but which at the same time deviate from or are irregular from the militia. "Paramilitary groups" are bodies which act together with the military institution but which at the same time exercise irregular action, deviated, deformed, from the military.

If the military institution has a role in society or in a state governed by laws, a State of Law, it is exactly that of exercising, in the name of and by delegation of the social body, the armed or war activity in defense of that same social body, within strict ethical and legal norms which impede it from departing from its dangerous role. If there is a justification for the existence of the institution, it is precisely the danger that someone who is not rigorously formed in the ethical and legal canons of the use of arms might have opportunity to use them, and above all that someone not be held rigorously accountable for his actions in the use of arms.

Both the politization or ideological conversion of men of arms, which leads them to use force in the defense of the interests of one group or sector of the society and not in defense of the interests of the community as a whole, and the practice of linking armed action to civilian persons or groups contradict the legitimizing principle of the armed forces of the state. In this last case, the armed forces lose their reason for being, since this is essentially conceived to be an exercise or action which cannot or ought not to be exercised by civilians. Therefore this tends to destroy the founding principles of the State of Law: equality of all those associated before the law and the illegitimacy of any citizens using force to submit others to their interests.

The denaturing of the military institution occurs when these departures from the norm are added together: the adopting of an ideology by ideolization of the armed forces and the blurring of the frontiers between what is civilian and what is military. But these departures reach the highest level of perversion when they are conditioned to mechanisms of secrecy, as subterfuges to make a mockery of their responsibilities. When one arrives at this level, the "State of Law" has ceased to exist.

* * *

The tendency to erase the borders between the civilian and the military has a long history in Colombia and has even been sought to be legalized by means of spurious processes.

Up to 1989, the legal substantiation for the proliferation of paramilitary civilian armed groups coordinated by the Army was found in paragraph 3 of Article 33 of Decree 3398 of 1965. This was converted into permanent legislation by Law 48 of 1968. This principle authorized the Ministry of National Defense "by conduct of authorized commanders to support, when it considers convenient, as if private property, arms which are considered as being of a private use of the Armed Forces." Besides this, in Article 25 the mentioned Decree authorizes the National Government to utilize the civilian population "in activities and works by which they contribute to the reestablishment of normality."

However, in a sentence of May 25, 1989, the Supreme Court declared unconstitutional Paragraph 3 of Article 33 of said Decree 3398 and explained what Article 25 covered. According to the Supreme Court, Paragraph 3 of Article 33 conflicted with the constitutional principle of a monopoly of arms of war being in the head of the government, "which is responsible for maintaining public order and for reestablishing it when it is disturbed."

This is a legal disposition which has, in addition, the Court observed, an "historical sense for resolving serious conflicts which affect civilian relations among Colombians and which now acquires a renewed significance in the face of problems which have brought about the diverse forms of the present violence."

With respect to Article 25, the Supreme Court explained that it is only "the National Government, working as such, the President and Minister of Defense, which can, by means of Decree, mobilize and utilize all Colombians in the task of reestablishing normality, when a cause of foreign war, commotion or public calamity presents itself."

The Court noted that "the interpretation of these norms has led to confusion in some sectors of public opinion which propose that they can be utilized as a legal authorization to organize civilian armed groups." But the Court itself is emphatic in concluding that "the activity of these groups is located at the margin of the Constitution and of the laws."

Notwithstanding the decision of the Court, high government counselors continued defending the "legality" of paramilitary groups, or groups of self-defense until 1989, with the pretense that their responsible persons not be tried in a judicial process.

The abusive interpretation of these norms was so audacious in the high military ranks that very soon internal resolutions began to appear tending to impel the involvement of the civilian population in armed actions. Resolution 005 of April 9, 1969 in its Article No. 183 is oriented toward "organizing in military form the civilian population, so that it will protect against the action of the guerrillas and will support the carrying out of combat operations."

Further along, the same resolution establishes the setting up of "self defense boards." These are defined as "an organization of military type which is made up of civilian personnel selected from the combat zone, which is trained and equipped to develop actions against groups of guerrillas who appear in the area or to operate in coordination with troops in actions of combat." These "self defense boards" also will be utilized to "prevent the formation of armed groups." The setting up, training and providing of arms to them are also considered in the resolution.

After the mentioned resolution, many others followed which promulgated rules of anti-guerrilla combat, where it was taken as given that the objective of the troops would be setting up of armed civilian groups and providing orientation to promote them. (See the Counter-Guerrilla Manual of 1979; the Manual of Combat Against Bandits or Guerrillas-Resolution 0014 of June 25, 1982, EJC-3-101/82; the Regulations of Counter-Guerrilla Combat-EJC-3-10/87).

But the linking of the civilian population to armed actions, which supposedly would be exclusively of active members of the public forces, obeys an unconfessable objective which becomes explicit in some of these "secret" manuals, thanks to its character of being clandestine: it hides the identity of agents of the State or allows them to carry out "covered up operations."

Paramilitarism becomes, then, the keystone of a strategy of "Dirty War," where the "dirty" actions cannot be attributed to persons on behalf of the State because they have been delegated, passed along or projected upon confused bodies of armed civilians. Those committing the crimes are anonymous and easily definable as common delinquents who act and thereafter disappear into the fog. This covers up responsibility for acts which have no legal justification or legitimacy, not even during times of warlike confrontations. The result is that they confound and complement two types of events: actions of military officers camouflaged as civilians and military action of civilians protected in a clandestine way by military personnel. Both types of procedures have the same objective: to provide impunity through cover ups.

* * *

The terrorist wave which was set loose in Bogota and in other regions of the country towards the end of 1978, after Decree 1923 became law—that Decree being better known as the Statute of Security—led to the identifying of an audacious form of "Terrorism of the State." In effect, beginning in September of 1978, phone and written threats were received by people known for their beliefs in democracy, including a high magistrate of the Court who objected to the constitutionality of the Statute of Security. Dynamite was used in attacks carried out against the headquarters of the Communist Party, against an afternoon newspaper of the capital city, and against a magazine. The kidnapping and "disappearance" of several activists of the left and of university leaders, were carried out by the underground "Triple A" (or "American Anti-Communist Action"). Later, the findings of the precarious investigative processes which were initiated and the confession of two deserters to a Bogota daily newspaper, led to the uncovering of agents whose identity was kept secret by the Triple A to military personnel attached to the "Battalion of Intelligence and Counter-Intelligence Charry Solano-BINCI." The names of the officials who were charged with these deeds would later on be familiar to the majority of Colombians, since they received all of the promotions and military honors possible and occupied the highest offices and responsibility in the hierarchy of the Colombian Armed Forces.

* * *

On December 3, 1981, a helicopter spread fliers over the City of Cali announcing publicly the establishing of the group MAS: "Death to Kidnappers" (Muerte a Secuestradores). The fliers mentioned that 223 chiefs of the Mafia (the "kidnapables") had joined together and had put up money to create a squadron of 2,230 men, which was to execute without mercy any person linked to any kidnapping. The fliers affirmed that "the kidnappers who were detained by the authorities will be executed in prison." They cited the case of Martha Nieves Ochoa, daughter of an Antioquian drug-trafficking leader, who was freed by MAS after her kidnapping by members of the M-19 guerrilla group.

The logo of MAS began to appear in diverse regions of the country, attributing to itself numerous crimes, disappearances, massacres, assassinations, attempts at assassination, and threats. A youth captured in Medellin in May of 1982 and brutally tortured in the installations of the B-2 one night was taken blindfolded to a private house to avoid having a search commission find him in the military quarters in which he had been tortured. Later, the house would be identified as that of Fabio Ochoa, which provided evidence of the close collaboration between drug traffickers and military officers in this type of covered-up operation.

The year 1982 was full of actions of MAS. Civilian armed groups in rural regions began to identify themselves with this logo, particularly in Caqueta and in the Middle Magdalena. There was no doubt that a strategy of private and clandestine justice had been mounted with the participation and support of the Armed Forces. The national and international movement in favor of human rights began to pressure the Betancur government to take a position with respect to this phenomenon and Betancur requested that the Attorney General investigate.

From October of 1982 on, eight criminal justices, accompanied by special prosecutors and by investigators of the judicial police, carried out investigations in Medellin, Cali, Barrancabermeja, Puerto Berrio, La Dorada, Puerto Boyaca and Arauca. On February 20, 1983, the Attorney General (Procurador General) made public a report about MAS with the names of 163 persons linked to this death squad, among them 59 active members of the public forces. In defining the phenomenon, the Attorney General affirmed:

> This deals purely and simply with government personnel who get out of line facing the temptations of multiplying their capacity of action and of taking advantage of private agents, whom they begin to take as "guides" and "informers," collaborators and helpers in general, and whom they end up using as a hidden arm so that a plan using them as hired killers is made unofficially which officially these personnel could not do.

The animated reaction of the Armed Forces toward the report led to fear of a coup and that is what the Minister of Defense of that time insinuated in an editorial of the *Magazine of the Armed Forces* (January, 1983):

> Arguments for a new internal conflict of the nation could be originating, since undoubtedly that honest part of society, which considers itself represented in a dignified manner and defended by the Armed Forces, would tend to stand up at the side of these institutions and the institutions, facing the perspective of the undermining of their dignity, could become of a mind for a struggle of incalculable and unforeseeable proportions which would take our country to a new phase of violence.

The Attorney General's office itself would adopt from that time on a favorable attitude toward paramilitarism, by abstaining from gathering evidence and by refusing to implement any sanctioning measure against the members of MAS. The country would tend to accustom itself from then on to the so strange policy of impunity which is covered under the name of an "Attorney General's Office of Opinion" (Procuraduria de Opinion).

The government did the same and abstained from discharging the accused from military service. Meanwhile, the Congress of the Republic approved promotions and honors for almost all of them. A retrospective reading of this lists shows that the State, by means of all its powers, conferred upon the members of MAS successively the highest responsibilities in the management of "public order" and the highest posts and honors in the military hierarchy. From then on, the paramilitary strategy was clearly shown, with the clearest signs that could be set forth in the mechanisms of social communication, as an uncompromising policy of the state.

* * *

The point of transition of command from President Julio Cesar Turbay to President Belisario Betancur in 1982 also signified a fundamental restructuring of the repressive policy of the state.

A high level evaluation, carried out within the Armed Forces, upon the effects of the repressive model which grew up around the Statute of Security (1978-1982), gave as a result a military failure (since subversion increased in alarming proportions during this period in which all had been designed for its definitive extermination) and a political failure (for the notable deterioration of the governing party as much at a national level as an international level).

Betancur designed, as a way out of this, talk of "peace" and of "negotiation." However the internal communications directed to the military high command by its high officers on June 25, 1992 and on May 1, 1994, provided evidence of the military's lack of agreement with this model and revealed an underground movement within the Public Forces in support of another strategy not made explicit.

But in one part of the country, disagreement with the "politics of peace" of Betancur was proclaimed loudly and a different alternative was pronounced, with pride and noise, as a solution to the conflict: an alliance between the Armed Forces and civilians in a counterinsurgency struggle. At the entrance to Puerto Boyaca a gigantic billboard was erected on which a "welcome" was extended to "the anti-Communist Capital of Colombia."

A coming together of powers and circumstances converted Puerto Boyaca into the "Vatican" of paramilitarism between 1982 and 1989: creation of the XIV Brigade of the Army and its placement in Cimitarra and later in Puerto Berrio (1982-83); assignment to that Brigade of the Barbula Battalion, located in Puerto Boyaca (1983); the mentality of the commanders of these units, infused completely with all of the principles of the Doctrine of National Security, as they explained it numerous times; the unrestricted support which their superior hierarchies gave them at the highest levels; the leadership of military and civilian mayors, who were originators of the project; the economic support of cattlemen of the zone and of other wealthy persons; the support of political leaders of the zone, favored by their liberal chiefs of ministerial rank; and abuses and extor-

tions by the XI Front of the FARC, guerrillas, which operated in the region.

The paramilitarism of Puerto Boyaca was converted
little by little into an undertaking of great strength. Soon
it changed its name from MAS to that of autodefensas
(self-defenses). It was organized as a network of armed
civilian groups, coordinated and trained by the army, in
a frenetic action of extermination of "communists."

The bombardments carried out by military helicopters were accompanied or followed by exterminating
incursions of the "Autodefensas," directed against
activists of any social or political organization of leftist
ideology. The arms were provided to them by the XIV
Brigade, as was publicly announced in the newspaper
Puerto Rojo, in its edition of August 1987: "The arms were
acquired in the XIV Brigade, undoubtedly by all persons
who needed them...." A legally registered organization,
ACDEGAM (The Peasant Association of Farmers and
Ranchers of the Middle Magdalena), channeled military
projects, "legally"—those which were financial, educa-
tional, sanitary, of infrastructure and of roads. By means
of these the "Autodefensas" sought to win and control
the entire population. Later a "legal" political movement
would seek to expand the experience as political ideology: MORENA (The Movement of National Renovation).

No one would be able to say that the diverse powers of the State did not back the paramilitary plan of
Puerto Boyaca. In the archives of the state there are to be
found at least four confessions which coincide and are
highly reliable:

1. On May 10, 1988, agents of the DAS drafted a
comprehensive document based upon the confessions of
Diego Viafara Salinas, who was a member of the City
Council of Puerto Boyaca between 1988 and 1990, but

who had been linked to the "Autodefensas" since 1983. Viafara detailed the participation of the Barbula Battalion in the paramilitary plan and its coordination with the Liberal Party politician Pablo Guarin, who was himself supported by the Minister of Government Jaime Castro, as was also his long work in health plans of ACDEGAM (page 7). Participation is viewed in the activities of ACDEGAM and the "Autodefensas" by recognized leaders of the paramilitaries or of drug trafficking of some other regions, such as Gonzalo Rodriguez Gacha, Fabio Ochoa, Fidel Castano, Victor Carranza and Pablo Escobar (page 8 and page 20). Viafara's statements also allege that the Barbula Battalion and the Autodefensas carried out patrols together (page 10).

The statement by Viafara also describes in detail circumstances in which the alliance between the "Autodefensas" and the drug traffickers began in 1985 (page 11) and the hiring of Israeli and English mercenaries to train the paramilitaries (page 19). It enumerates the places in the country where the "Autodefensas" had been established (pages 24-26), and these coincided with the large number of reports which had been presented about the presence of paramilitary groups attached to the Armed Forces. Viafara's statement amply tells of the development of the relations between paramilitarism and drug-trafficking and the mechanisms used to undermine investigations about crimes which they commit (pages 50 and following).

2. In November 1989, the Dijin of Bogota interrogated Luis Antonio Meneses Baez, who had been captured for other suspicious activities, and drafted another profoundly revealing document which contains his confessions. Meneses reveals there that the commanders of the Brigade and of the Battalion (XIV Brigade and the

Barbula Battalion) linked him to the "Autodefensas" of Puerto Boyaca in 1981, at a time when he was an officer of the army. He affirms that "the peasant autodefensas...are a policy of the Government for the counter-insurgency struggle" (page 4). Later, the II Brigade, with headquarters in Barranquilla, gave him the task of creating other "Autodefensas" in the south of Bolivar. The B-2 of the Brigade established the link between the "Autodefensas" and the military hierarchies and the arms which were provided by Indumil (the government military provisions office) (pages 5 and 6). When in 1987 the "Autodefensas" saw the necessity of integrating themselves on a national level,

> military intelligence led by the Charry Solano Battalion brought together peasant self-defense movements under their control and to do that they organized a meeting with the regional leaders in the buildings of the Charry, where a National Self-Defense Board arose, composed of leaders of approximately eight regions, whose function was to promote the system of self-defense and to coordinate with army intelligence operations (page 7).

Three national meetings are talked about: one in the Charry Solano Battalion in 1986; another in Santander in 1987; and another in September of 1989 in the rural area of Caqueta (pages 10-11). The organization possessed a military chief, who "coordinated the mixed operations of a military type with the Armed Forces" (page 11). There are enumerated 22 fronts of "Autodefensas," which coincide with the recognized focus points of paramilitarism in the country (pages 15-17); in each front the "Commander or military person in charge" "coordinates with the Self-Defense board and the Armed Forces the operations and activities to be carried out (page 18). With respect to patrolling, Meneses's statement alleges that normally it is mixed (Armed Forces-Autodefensas), based upon techniques imparted by the Army...when the Autodefensas is alone, it is informed of the movements of military units or of the Police which can be made aware of its activity (page 22).

Meneses Baez establishes in his confession that there is a certain change in emphasis which occurs in the relations between the Armed Forces and the "Autodefensas" in 1989: "Until the beginning of 1989, the contacts were made with the High Command of the Army and now intermediaries are utilized..."(page 24).

3. In 1990, the DAS (Administrative Department of Security) drafted another document with the confession of Army Major Oscar de Jesus Echandia Sanchez, who had been the military mayor of Puerto Boyaca between 1981 and 1982 and a co-founder of the MAS. He retired from the army in 1988, when an order of capture calling for the assassination of the Mayor of Sabana de Torres weighed upon him, but he was protected by the command of the VIII Brigade, continuing attached as a retired military officer to paramilitarism until his confession in 1990, when he became an informant of the DAS.

Major Echandia told with chilling casualness of the killing of "communists" and even of "galanistas" (followers of Luis Carlos Galan, a Liberal Party leader) in the Middle Magdalena, referring to about 300 assassinations (pages 6,7, 10). The historical conjuncture in which the alliance between paramilitarism and drug trafficking was produced is pointed out, 1983-84 (page 8). He denounces the close relationship existing between the Commander of the School of Cavalry of the Army, Colonel Plazas Vega, and the "Autodefensas" of drug trafficker Rodriguez Gacha (page 9). Major Echandia's story uncovers the originating relationship which the paramilitary structure of

Puerto Boyaca had with other paramilitary structures which later on were developed scandalously, such as those of San Juan Bosco de La Verde and the Chucurena region and those of Uraba and Cordoba commanded by Fidel Castano (page 11). Major Echandia's statement tells of the hiring of English and Israeli mercenaries for the training of the paramilitaries in 1989 (page 14 and following) and affirms that "always when foreign persons visited Puerto Boyaca, especially mercenaries, they arrived accompanied by a convoy of agents of the F-2 or civilian personnel of the army" (page 20).

4. When in 1989, Colonel Luis Arcenio Bohorquez Montoya, commander of the Barbula Battalion of Puerto Boyaca, was called upon to end his military service after word of the scandal had been released about the presence of foreign mercenaries who trained paramilitary group members, this official made public a letter to the Minister of Defense in which reference was made to the former directors of the highest military officialdom linked to the creation of the self-defense groups, directorships which extended up to the highest hierarchies. The officer indicated he did not understand why he was punished since he had limited himself to following the orientation of his superiors in the hierarchy. (Cite to the daily newspaper "La Prensa," October 15, 1989, page 5).

* * *

The paramilitary experience of Puerto Boyaca was, thus, profoundly revealing. The diverse confessions which revealed its structures and practices permit the sketching of its fundamental characteristics:

- Financial support on the part of the trade organizations and powerful businesses: large agricultural producers, cattlemen, oil companies, and later drug-trafficking led by its most recognized leaders;

- Political support of military and civilian mayors, of leaders of the traditional parties whose line of "cacique-style leadership" penetrated up to the Congress and to the high Executive Power by means of sponsoring ministers;

- Military support in the local battalion which at the same time obtained its support from the respective brigade arriving at the high command of the Army to coordinate at the moment of expansion of the experience, the National Self-Defense Board through the Charry Solano Battalion; (It needs to be added that the international military support through the English and Israeli mercenaries were escorted to Puerto Boyaca by public forces, and also enjoyed immunity within their own countries).

- Highly effective support by the judicial power, which absolved the responsible parties or tabled the poor criminal proceedings which had been opened on the occasion of hundreds of crimes committed by the paramilitary structure. And when the courts sentenced some person involved in these crimes to punishment for them, they refused to investigate and judge the lines of command and the criminal structure itself;

- Extremely effective support by the Executive and Legislative powers, which, in spite of the publicity of the names of those who set up and directed this criminal structure, provided distinction to those responsible with all kinds of promotions in rank and honors which the military hierarchy and tradition provided for;

- Remarkably effective support by the organisms of control of the state, which abdicated voluntarily their powers to punish wrongdoers upon finding themselves face to face with this paramilitary phenomenon.

* * *

Then in 1987, the scandalous development of paramilitarism began to be a point of public debate. In September of that year, the debate reached Congress and there many positions were made explicit: The Minister of Defense, General Rafael Samudio, confessed himself in favor of the "Autodefensas"; he was accompanied by generals and former generals, former Ministers and political leaders, predominantly conservatives, as well as leaders of powerful economic trade organizations.

The years 1988 and 1989, marked by an impressive number of massacres which made history, attributed to the paramilitaries, sharpened the debate. It was, however, when dialogue with some guerrilla groups began that the "legal" status of the paramilitaries came to be defined. In effect, some sectors of the M-19, facing the prospect of a transfer to a legal status, found in the government's predominant interpretation of Article 33 of Law 48 of 1968 a possibility of continuing as an armed group but "within the bounds of legality."

M-19 leaders suggested to the governmental negotiators that the Minister of Defense provide them with safe conduct passes for the use of arms designed for private use by the Armed Forces, so as to constitute themselves as "Autodefensas" in the style of those already "legally" existing, supported, promoted, and protected by the public forces.

President Barco was pressured, then, using his powers under the "State of Siege," to issue a decree suspending the provisions of Paragraph 3 of Article 33 of Law 48 of 1968 (Decree 815, of April 19, 1989). Later, the Supreme Court would declare this norm to be "unconstitutional" (after tolerating it for 30 years!), but it would leave clear that the civilian armed groups never had been legal, since with the two controversial articles still existing, nothing authorized their interpretation as legalizing groups of armed civilians.

Barco issued other complementary decrees "against paramilitarism": he created an advisory commission to coordinate the struggle against paramilitarism (Decree 813 of 1989) and a special armed body to combat paramilitary groups (Decree 814 of 1989). Besides this a Barco decree classified promotion or participation in these groups "wrongly called paramilitary groups" as a crime (Decree 1194 of 1989).

With these measures apparently paramilitarism became illegal. However, it is known that the advisory commission (called "Commission Against Hired Killings") met only once, only to justify its existence. Its one meeting had no real importance, and the supposed armed body to combat paramilitarism never existed. The judicial power, on its part, never has come to condemn anyone for paramilitarism. The only intent to capture some paramilitary persons, on March 29, 1992 in El Carmen de Chucurí, was impeded by an illegal military threat whose authors were never themselves punished either. We must remember here that Luis Antonio Meneses Baez in his confession had pointed out that "until 1989 contacts were made with the high command of the army and now intermediaries are utilized" (page 24).

A change came about, thus, in paramilitarism in the period of time around 1989: the shrill and audacious public cycle of the model of Puerto Boyaca had ended. From then on, paramilitarism would not be recognized explicitly by the government; it would pass to the condition of a clandestine prostitute, but its actions would not be diminished on that account. On the contrary, supported by secrecy it would become even stronger.

* * *

The paramilitary complex of Puerto Boyaca, as it is described in three more extensive confessions, was projected onto various regions of the country where important paramilitary focus areas were created. One of these was the region of Uraba and the south of Cordoba, where Fidel Castano Gil would become the paramilitary's principal leader (see Viafara, pages 8 and 20; Meneses, pages 15-17; Echandia, page 11).

Echandia states that

> In 1988...it became known that Gonzalo and Henry Perez had bought properties in Uraba and that by the order of Pablo Escobar and Gonzalo Rodriguez Gacha they organized a "cleansing" of the part of Uraba that is in Antioquia. The massacres in Uraba began then. Participating as the leaders were N.N. (alias Fercho), a former member of the Ricardo Franco Front of the FARC, and Fidel Castano Gil. While Luis Rubio was Mayor of Puerto Boyaca, he coordinated the transportation of the hired killers to Uraba.

On April 4, 1990, another paramilitary group member, this one in the service of Fidel Castano, made a confession before the DAS and told the details of some massacres: that of 42 peasants in Pueblo Bello (Turbo, Antioquia, in January of 1990); that of the small settlement Villavicencio (Valencia, Cordoba, in October of 1988); and that of Pueblo Bujo (Monteria, in November of 1989). He also told of the assassinations of Alfonso Ospina and of Father Sergio Restrepo, S.J., in Tierralta (in June of 1989). According to Rogelio de Jesus Escobar, the hired killers of Castano, at that time around 100 in number, had as the center of their training the hacienda Las Tangas (Valencia, Cordoba), which he owned.

A former soldier testified in 1992 that at that hacienda only simulations of "searches" were carried out, since only commanders entered the hacienda and afterwards they left with boxes of liquor, cigarettes, canned goods and soft drinks to serve a banquet to the soldiers at the entrance to the hacienda. The same soldier affirms that some vehicles which were seen in the hacienda were seen frequently at the XI Brigade in Monteria. This testimony was "disappeared" by the Technical Unit of the Judicial Police. Escobar, in his confession, reveals the close relations between Castano and the Mayor of Monteria and describes how "the Police Station of Valencia had at its disposal a frequency to communicate with the organization of Fidel Castano, advising it in opportune fashion of the presence of suspects or of the carrying out of operations in the farms of the paramilitary group" (page 33).

* * *

Another of the paramilitary structures which originated in the complex in Puerto Boyaca, but which would take its own shape, and, in this case, would be converted into a pet pilot project of the high military command, is the paramilitary project of the Chucurena zone in Santander.

The confession of Echandia relates how

> in 1987...Henry Perez asked that 10 peasants be selected from the hamlet of San Juan Bosco de La Verde in the jurisdiction of Santa Helena del Opon (Santander), in order to participate in a course of combat in the jurisdiction of Puerto Boyaca. After the course the peasants returned to San Juan Bosco armed with weapons and equipped with war materiel and radios (page 11).

And previously, supported by the Operative Command No. 10 of the Army with headquarters in Cimitarra (precursor of the XIV Brigade later established in Puerto Berrio), the first paramilitary base had been created in San Juan Bosco de La Verde in 1981. Other confessions which we found in the Annales of the Congress (Year XXVI, No. 104, October 4, 1983, pages 1508 and following) relate how the commander of the Operative Command No. 10 went in military helicopters to train paramilitaries. Puerto Boyaca later invited the paramilitaries of San Juan Bosco de La Verde to come to receive better training.

From San Juan Bosco de La Verde, this paramilitary structure was expanded to the municipalities of El Carmen and San Vicente de Chucurí (1986-1995) and spread in the later years into nearby municipalities: Betulia, Simacota, Galan, Zapatoca, Barrancabermeja, Sabana de Torres and Puerto Wilches. The characteristics which this experience was acquiring converted it into a pilot project for the Armed Forces.

The compulsory involvement of all of the population in armed conflict has been sought, so as to render any position of neutrality impossible within the controlled territory. At the same time, the leaders of this project have sought to make it highly self-financing, by collecting extortionate taxes from the population. There are only three alternatives which are left to the peasant: collaborate with paramilitarism and submit himself to its impositions; abandon the zone; or die. Since 1987, more than 300 residents of El Carmen, who did not wish to submit themselves nor to emigrate, have been assassinated and close to 4,000 have preferred to abandon the zone.

Those who remain must build paramilitary bases; they must deliver up their young children to paramilitary training and patrols by turns; they must pay taxes for the sustaining of the group; and they are required to attend every meeting. The coordination between the military and the paramilitiaries here is revealing: the paramilitary bases are built close to military bases. Meetings are called by the military and are presided over by paramilitary leaders or vice versa. Census data collected by the military appear in the hands of the paramilitary, or vice versa. Persons captured by the military are delivered over to the paramilitaries. And military and paramilitary commanders go about together to stores and houses collecting the "taxes."

Such a collapsing of all legality only would be conceivable with a thick cover of secrecy, but in this case there are more than 10 years of intense and documented reports. This is perhaps the clearest test made of the justice system, providing evidence of its complicity with paramilitarism. When one Regional Judge ordered the capture of 26 paramilitary personnel of the zone, military officers impeded the capture by means of an illegal threat. The Attorney General (Fiscal General) then brought the case to his office, put at liberty those few paramililtary personnel who had been detained and controlled closely the report on the incident to manage it with the evident goals of coverup and impunity.

The pilot experiment of paramilitarism in the Santander Zone of Chucurí has another ingredient which assures its success: management of the mass media. After the frustrated attempt at making effective the 26 orders of capture issued by one Regional Attorney General—a really outrageous case within the type of behavior of the judicial apparatus facing paramilitarism—the military officers went to the mass media to fabricate a false image of what had really happened. They had two purposes in mind which could not be disguised: to hide the crimes committed there by the state/parastate and to stigmatize before public opinion those who denounced what was happening there. The newspapers "El Tiempo" and "La Prensa" and radio station "R.C.N." fulfilled these goals by means of the most anti-ethical fabrications and manipulations. The target of these very dirty procedures were the parish priest of El Carmen de Chucurí, one of the leaders of the Base Communities of El Carmen, and the Commission of Justicia y Paz.

The strategy of stigmatizing those who provided information concerning the activities of paramilitary from then on patently involved the mechanisms of personal ties of the paramilitary. The Attorney General's office, by all accounts pressured by military officers, by paramilitary leaders and by journalists who are in league with them, issued an Order of Capture against the parish priest of El Carmen and against "the sacristan," thanks to gratuitous "accusations" which in no other country would have any validity (persons linked to paramilitarism brought to Cucuta in military helicopters to tell before a "Faceless Judge" that the Father "did" or "said" something, without any reference to dates, places or circumstances which could be checked, without any witness and with numerous contradictions). But these accusations did serve their purpose in getting the mass "information" media to make profuse use of them to convince the country that the parish priest was a "guerrilla" and that, for that reason, his denunciation of paramilitarism was a "lie."

The confession of the Commander of the Police of El Carmen de Chucurí before the Office of the Procurador in November of 1992 revealed the mechanisms of coordination which operated between the army and the paramilitaries: they had planned to assassinate the parish priest, the city clerk and several members of the Communal Action Board on the night of October 4, 1992, but the Commander of the police failed them at the last moment, disobeying the order to keep all of his men in the barracks, opting rather to defend the victims. The failure of this attempt led to the persecution by other means of the parish priest, as has already been shown.

The confession of Gonzalo Ortega Parada in August of 1987 before the office of the Procurador has uncovered also the connections which existed between the Ricaurte Battalion of the V Brigade and the paramilitary organizations of San Juan Bosco de La Verde. Hired to assassinate the Mayor of Sabana de Torres in August of 1987, Ortega refused to do it and deserted from his job as an informant and as a civilian hitman of the army. He revealed the participation of the paramilitary group of San Juan Bosco de La Verde in the crime, coordinated by the Ricaurte Battalion. Defining his work as a paramilitary person, Ortega stated:

> Other civilians worked on special missions, almost always reservists, because we have a military mentality, but we are not in active service. And thus if something goes awry, nothing can be proven as far as active military personnel are concerned. (Report in the magazine *Cromos*, September, 1987.)

* * *

Another of the paramilitary structures which appear as mentioned in the three key confessions about Puerto Boyaca is the structure of Victor Carranza, whose paramilitary empire has extended through the Departments of Meta, Vichada, Guainia, Casanare and Boyaca. Some of his men participated in the training given by foreign mercenaries and in some instances coordinated activities. (See Viafara, pages 8/20; Meneses, pages 15/17; Echandia, page 11.)

The confession of Camilo Zamora Guzman, given before the Fourth Court of Public Order of Villavicencio on April 10 and 11, 1989, is a chilling document which reflects the psychology of the hired killer, whose profitable business is death, a business which fills with a lethal coldness the extensive narrative of a genocide, seemingly without so many and such horrible crimes even disturbing his sleep.

Throughout these 20 pages, the curtain is drawn back which covers numerous crimes in the eastern part of the country and allows us to see, as if through a surprise hole, the machinery—still running—which allows us to realize the genocide of the Patriotic Union.

Another confession given in the jail of Villavicencio at the beginning of 1995 by a person in the paramilitary organization of Carranza, reveals in full action the machinery of death which Zamora paints in 1989. In one of its passages, it describes in this way the routine procedures:

> The "autodefensas" and their commanders inform the Police and the Army about the class of "work" which they are going to carry out, in great detail, then on the day and at the hour decided upon the uniformed persons come together; when they are going to carry out a job in a locality...then a police officer comes and goes ahead of the vehicles of the "autodefensas." And he has the numbers of the license plates of these cars, so at the police checkpoints there is no problem for the cars to go through. In the cars of the "autodefensas," it is understood, go the arms (page 2).

* * *

The XIV Brigade of the army, with its headquarters in Puerto Berrio, Antioquia was, from its beginnings, a focus of paramilitarism. It could be inferred that its very foundation was due to these hidden purposes. The Barbula Battalion of Puerto Boyaca belonged to its command; and it participated in the founding, coordination, and maintaining of the most audacious and public paramilitary project, already described.

The confession of Martin Emiliol Sanchez Rodriguez, given before delegates of the Archbishop of Medellin on May 3, 1990 and later before the Office of Special Investigations of the Procuraduria General of the Nation on June 21, 1990, permits one to glimpse another chilling chain of crimes sponsored from the XIV Brigade and to penetrate into the structures of the GRUPO HURE (Hure Group), an authentic paramilitary structure linked to the XIV Brigade, to which the witness belonged. There, the assassinations of Father Jaime Restrepo (in Providencia, San Roque, in January of 1988) and of a nun of the Company of Maria, Teresita Ramirez (Cristales, in February of 1989), are revealed, as are other numerous crimes of this region.

When in 1992 the Commission of Justice and Peace (Justicia y Paz) presented before the Attorney General (Fiscal) of the nation and before the Minister of National Defense new well-founded evidence that the assassins had come from the XIV Brigade, members of which had carried out numerous attempts against the Peasant Refuge of Barrancabermeja—a humanitarian service for peasant victims of state-sponsored violence in the Middle Magdalena region—the Attorney General abdicated his investigative faculties and limited himself to carrying out the role of "good offices" before the minister. And the minister himself refused absolutely to take note of the evidence, in spite of the fact that much of it was based on investigations carried out on diverse occasions in different places and at different times. Later, the Procurador's office decided to "table" the investigation about the attempts against the Refuge without investigating them, and it limited itself to seeking to find out the author of the murder of an informant of the paramilitaries (who had been sought in a derivative form) avoiding investigation of the chain of attempts against the Refuge.

* * *

The confession of Meneses Baez identified Cesar as another focus of paramilitarism (page 15). Since 1989, the National Directorate of Criminal Instruction there had received chilling testimonies about what had occurred on the hacienda Riverandia, of San Alberto in Cesar, property of the family of a member of parliament (Rivera). There on November 4, 1988, two youths were introduced violently into the hacienda by a group of armed civilians, discovering in the interior a camp of the army, and they were victims of torture and an attempt at crucifixion (one of the youths was assassinated when attempting to escape). The owners of the hacienda, the military officers and the group of hired civilian killers acted in unison, using civilian vehicles and civilian dress to perpetrate their crimes.

Various small towns of Cesar have suffered the permanent flagellation of paramilitarism, which has produced in this region numerous victims since 1988. San Alberto, San Martin and Aguachica have been its principal centers of operations. In January of 1995, investigations initiated by the massacre of Puerto Patino (Aguachica) were placed into evidence, thanks to a confession of another member of the public forces, the para-military structure which operates there, directed by the very commander of the military base of Aguachica him-self, Major Jorge A. Lazaro.

* * *

Though since 1984/85 paramilitarism has made multiple alliances with important sectors of drug traf-ficking, in the Department of Valle del Cauca these two phenomena have marched along together.

The massacres of Trujillo, (1988/1994), and Riofrio (1993) in the center of Valle, as well as that which occurred in Cali in April of 1992, uncovered paramilitary structures linked to drug trafficking which operated there and their coordination with military units and police units. One of the units which stand out is the Palace Battalion with its headquarters in Buga.

The Commission of Investigation of the Violent Events of Trujillo, which acted within the structure of the gestures carried forward by the Inter-American Commission of Human Rights, uncovered the responsi-bility of members of the Palace Battalion in carrying out the Trujillo massacre and in its coordination with a wide network of hired killers who worked in the service of two powerful drug traffickers of the region.

It also uncovered the procedures of secrecy tending to cover up the responsibility of the agents of the state. Among these were the use of private haciendas and vehicles for detentions and tortures, of civilian dress, and of bogus or hidden license plates. Other procedures used were a non-registration of those detained; verbal orders for operations absolutely illegal and criminal; hiding and mutilation of the cadavers; and the intimida-tion of witnesses and family members. The police Commands of Trujillo, Tulua, Riofrio and Buga linked all of these mechanisms together, in close coordination with the army and with the drug traffickers and their hitmen, to assure the "success" of the crimes.

All this leads us to believe that the genocide which has been practiced in Cali for the last several years against the juvenile population of the marginal neighborhoods follows the same parameters of paramilitarism.

The money of the Cartel of Cali, which has permeated and corrupted the police structures of the city—which is public knowledge—has served, in this way, to pay death squadrons infiltrated into these very same neighborhoods, who assassinate youths under justification of "social cleansing." Paramilitary groups, which are identified from the underground as "Cali Linda" (Beautiful Cali) or "Cali Limpia" (Clean Cali), enjoy the most absolute impunity and act with the overlooking and tolerance which are provided to them by the immense network of police checkpoints which crisscross the marginalized communities of the city.

* * *

Another recognized focal point of paramilitarism has been the Putumayo and its development in that region has been linked also to drug trafficking. In the zone of the great laboratories of cocaine, the drug traffickers have made an alliance, paradoxically, with the Anti-Narcotics Police, which control and protect the powerful paramilitary structure in the region.

During the years 1989 and 1990, the Lower Putumayo lived a blood bath. The army, the Anti-Narcotics Police and "Los Masetos" (a paramilitary group) acted in a coodinated manner and jointly in a demented and continuous massacre, especially of peasant youths, who just because of their age were accused of being "guerrillas," causing their death with no consequences for the killers.

The cadavers, tossed into rivers with those few rescued buried clandestinely, impeded the initiation even of an "investigation." When during Holy Week of 1991 the population of Puerto Asis exploded and went out into the streets to protest about the genocide, the police escorted "Pablo" to the airport, he being one of the principal local leaders of paramilitarism, before the protesters could lynch him.

The enormous lists of the dead who had been buried "canonically" through the Church (a very small percentage of the real victims), moved the Procurador General to present the case to the Director General of the Police in order to request of him emergency measures. The high official decided, as a contribution to the solution of the problem, to reassign to other areas immediately all of the personnel of the paramilitary institution there quartered. (Would they not go to "continue their work" in other latitudes?) Notwithstanding the testimony provided, among which was that of a miraculous survivor of one of the routine nocturnal massacres, no "investigation" ended up with a conviction. The perceptible recession in the criminal action of paramilitarism in the Putumayo during 1992 and 1993 appears to have arrived at its end. From the end of 1994 on, reactivation is evident.

* * *

But the essence of paramilitarism is not found only in groups of armed civilians. The action of the public forces "under civilian cover" (*sub specie civili*) also becomes the essence of paramilitarism insofar as it erases the visible frontiers between that which is civilian and that which is military, denaturalizing in that fashion the very legitimation of the military institution and perverting its very objectives, eluding responsibility for its acts before the community by hiding its identity. This perversion of object is especially clear where acts are done to perpetrate or cover up crimes which the military should by reason of their office rather have impeded.

The confession of First Vice Sergeant Alfonso Garzon Garzon, who for 20 years was linked to the Intelligence and Counter-Intelligence Battalion Charry Solano, later converted into the XX Brigade of Intelligence and Counter-Intelligence, given before the Office of Special Investigations of the Procurador General of the Nation on January 22 and 23, 1991, constitutes an impressive window which provides a view of systematic practices of the highest criminality in that institution. This confession was so overwhelming that it permitted the discovery of the mortal remains of some of the victims which confirmed those details of their revelations. As early as 1978, some deserters of the Binci had reported the foundation of the "Triple A" by high officials of the Binci Battalion, as well as some of the crimes which were perpetrated under that acronym. The total connivance of all of the powers of State has been the most effective support so that from that institution crimes continued to be perpetrated endlessly "*sub specie civili*," until the most recent of them was consummated in Bogota on March 28, 1995, with the assassination of Carlos Reyes Nino and Edgar Grimaldo in the shopping center Plaza de Las Americas, abandoning in that place a motorcycle registered to the XX Brigade.

The confession which Ricardo Gamez Mazuera provided on August 1, 1989 to the Office of the Procurador General of the Nation in his capacity as a former agent of the police and of the DIJIN (1974-77) and a former intelligence agent of the army command (1978-1989), constitutes another chilling testimony of the systematic criminal practices carried out *"sub specie civili"* by the intelligence organizations of the Public Forces. Throughout 17 pages of this confession, numerous curtains are opened to reveal the authorship and circumstances of crimes which left profound footprints on the national history: the deeds of the Palace of Justice and what became of some of those who disappeared there and the assassination of the Belgian Assumptionist priest Daniel Gillard in Cali.

Uncovered before the reader are death squads which made history in Tulua; unidentified graves which are the resting place for numerous victims of military and paramilitary action in Cucuta, Monteria, Bogota and the Eastern Plains; and "secret" negotiations between drug traffickers and military officers. The arsenal of concrete data and the very specific and sometimes graphic description of zones and places are impressive, but what is even more impressive is the overwhelming impunity with which all of the powers of state protect the numerous persons responsible for crimes.

One receives the same impression upon reading the text of the confession made by Lt. Nestor Eduardo Porras, of the National Police, before the Second Judge of Criminal Instruction in Facatativa on November 22, 1990. What is most impressive is the multitude of crimes narrated rapidly in these 6 pages, perpetrated by the DIJIN of Medellin in association with the Elite Force, of the army, corresponding just to the period January through May of 1990. It is like an instantaneous photograph which provides access to an orgy of blood which takes place in a den of iniquity.

Other revealing texts are the confessions of Saul Segura Palacios and of Carlos David Lopez, members of the 7th Network of Intelligence of the National Navy, given before the national attorney general's office, and later before other governmental offices in 1994. All these elements of military action *"sub specie civili"* for corrupt purposes are here brought together: civilian offices which are a facade (a store and an office of engineers); a network of hitmen or paid assassins to whom the crimes are entrusted; pseudonyms which identify all the way from the commanding colonel down to each one of the hitmen; payments to informants and to hitmen by means of "reserve funds" of the navy. This monstrous machinery of death underlay more than half a hundred crimes which caused consternation throughout the Middle Magdalena and the whole country.

* * *

At the initiation of the government of President Samper in August of 1994, paramilitarism had been fully consolidated, not only through its prolonged stages of development (beginning in 1968), but also because it had overcome all the obstacles to establish itself as a policy of the state.

Paramilitarism had undergone a great crisis in 1989, when the climax of the questioning of its legal status was reached, consigning it to a formally "illegal" existence. However, at that time the amazing practical intelligence of its initiators and promoters gave it different characteristics and it found a new status which permitted it to survive without losing strength. On the contrary, it demonstrated renewed dynamism which allowed it to overcome the obstacles which appeared "serious."

One asks oneself how a policy formally "illegal" can subsist with so much dynamism in a state which is said to be "of law." The reply need not be sought in legal texts, but rather in concrete and routine practices of the diverse powers, offices and institutions which make up the state.

- The military establishment, whose irregular projection is precisely paramilitarism, beginning in 1989 stopped defending publicly the legitimacy or "legality" of paramilitarism. But at the same time it consolidated throughout all of the country its relations, now clandestine or "intermediated" (according to the confession of Meneses Baez), with the networks of armed civilians already established from prior periods and created many other new ones. When some of those structures suffered excessive publicity or denunciation, they were considered to involve "isolated conduct" of an "insubordinate" official.

- For its part, the Executive Power ritualized its "condemnation" of paramilitarism in its speeches, especially in those directed toward international organizations, meanwhile calling to the highest command posts those strongest promoters of paramilitarism and providing promotions and honors to all of those who supported the paramilitaries. An integral part of their discourse was the routine public request to judicial and disciplinary powers to carry out "exhaustive investigations" about the paramilitaries, while at the same time abdicating ad hoc their authority to freely nominate and remove government officials for the purpose of guaranteeing a clean public administration.

- The Legislative Power, for its part, approved all of the promotions and honors for those who supported paramilitarism and passed laws and decrees of disguised amnesty and of judicial privilege applicable to whatever paramilitary group member might "by error" be submitted to investigation or trial (see Law 104 of 1993, Article 9; Code of Criminal Procedure, Article 369 A, B).

- But the wall of protection for paramilitarism built by all of the powers of the state has a central column, which is the Judicial Power.

According to the Administrative Department of National Planning, only 3% of the crimes reported in Colombia result in a conviction. Within this 3%, there has never been an investigation referring to a paramilitary structure. Thanks to this, presidents in their speech can confidently "legitimate" their position before the national and international community, seeking "exhaustive investigations" about paramilitarism, since their position is buttressed by the solid conviction that the opening of an investigation will certainly be formalized, but also the certainty that this will sink and disappear sooner or later, in the "black hole" of impunity.

Forgetting for the moment about military privilege and the structures of penal military "justice" already sufficiently diagnosed within and outside the country as a most effective mechanism of impunity, and leaving aside also for the moment the innumerable mechanism of impunity of the ordinary and regional jurisdictions focused upon in other studies, paramilitarism has enjoyed in the judicial realm extraordinary privileges because of its impunity.

The principal of these is the secrecy which characterizes the crimes of paramilitarism, which from the beginning impedes identification of those who carry out the crimes. But we are not talking here about just any secrecy, such as that which could protect a common criminal. What we are talking about is a secrecy which is protected or "escorted" by agents and/or institutions of the state. It is secrecy which occurs when civilians in the service of soldiers "or soldiers in the service of civilians" perpetrate crimes, often submitting their victims to the force of the "authority of the state" (always difficult or impossible to prove), but using private means (haciendas, vehicles, dress) to consummate the crime. It is secrecy which one realizes the perpetrators of the crimes enjoy, according to the particular case military or police control of the scene of the crime, a control which immobilizes resistance or the intent to report the crimes, or of a total clearing of the scene, when those who carry out the crime control it by themselves and can flee slowly and without any resistance. That secrecy creates the basic conditions of impunity, so that the Judicial Power can play its role.

The Judicial Power is asked not to take into account those specific mechanisms of secrecy officially "escorted," and to investigate deeds within legal and normal parameters: to look for written orders of search or capture (which do not exist); registries of those detained and of the control of vehicles in the minute books (which do not exist either); to interrogate witnesses who did not see or hear anything; to listen to "free and spontaneous declarations" by the very persons who carried out the crimes; to make relatives, neighbors and friends responsible for "not giving information."

These rituals having been practiced, there is inexorably declared a "lack of evidence," legitimating the finding of innocence or the tabling of the case. If by some accident a heroic witness turns up, then there are multiple methods foreseen for destroying that evidence: the threat of death (many times carried out); questioning the moral probity of the person, whether by looking for help from the Institute of Legal Medicine to declare him "mentally perturbed" (a resource which turned out to be key in the massacre of Trujillo and which still maintains absolute impunity of all of its authors), or be it accusing him of being a sympathizer with or collaborator of the guerrillas, and even opening up a criminal proceeding for that "crime" by means of declarations of "faceless witnesses" or of unconditional ones of paramilitarism, arriving at the extreme of issuing an order to capture for that reason (which was the case of the parish priest of El Carmen de Chucurí); or simply disqualifying the witnesses because they would be "interested in the case" (as occurred with the 24 witnesses of the assassination of the Swiss missionary Hildegard Feldmann).

Thus the Judicial Power has been the spinal column of the wall of protection of paramilitarism, and it is the Judicial Power which creates the most basic conditions permitting the military structure to continue projecting itself through this corrupted body, which enjoys the vital substance of the state sucked out by channels astutely hidden, and which at the same time makes possible the speech of the Executive formally "condemning" paramilitarism, remitting it to "exhaustive investigations" and processes of "justice," at the same time as he raises to the highest posts those who are authors and promoters of paramilitarism, at the same time "absolved" by "justice" or benefited by the routine filing of the evidence without acting on it.

The Office of the Attorney General, for its part, has adopted the same "investigative" and "proof gathering" mechanisms as the Judicial Power, providing a monstrous impunity also in the disciplinary field. Since Attorney General Jimenez Gomez in 1983 made public a list of the members of MAS at the same time as he exonerated them from disciplinary proceedings and punishment, defining his role as the "Procuraduria of Opinion," his successors have become accustomed to not investigating, processing or punishing, abdicating the disciplinary power which the constitution assigns them. Internal and external pressures have led them, in sum, to adopt the strategy of finding scapegoats (which can be counted on the fingers of one hand and are of the lowest rank), abstaining from investigating structures and chains of command.

The Samper government acts on top of this pedestal or with this backdrop. Its support for paramilitarism made things as easy as could be for it: it only had to leave things as they were, adopting the condemnatory speech of its predecessors and continuing to request "exhaustive investigations" of the judicial and disciplinary powers. But the Samper government did not choose this way. Near the end of the first year of its administration it can be proven that its position toward paramilitarism has not been limited to passive support, which could consist of reaping the benefits from the path built up during more than a decade with the collaboration of all of the offices of the state apparatus.

A few days after he had taken possession as Chief of State, President Samper made public, on September 9, 1994, a document which set forth his policy on human rights. Point No. 5 referred to paramilitarism and defined it as a phenomenon "linked, to a great degree, to the "territorialization" of a certain portion of drug trafficking funds which debilitate the legitimate monopoly of force which the state ought to maintain," and also as "a phenomenon, very much circumscribed, of formation of peasant "self-defense groups" (autodefensas) as a reaction to the attacks of "subversives."

No mention of the preponderant role which the State played (and specifically the Executive Power through the highest offices of the Public Forces) in the creation and organization of the paramilitary group. Nor has mention been made of the role as rector which they continue to carry out, with relative secrecy in the most varied places of the country, nor of the protection, support, weight, tolerance and collaboration which the different powers of the state have provided to paramilitarism by means of effective de facto mechanisms when not by formally "condemnatory" speeches which cover up practices contrary to law.

What does this "diagnostic" of paramilitarism seek to do? Certainly not to attempt to combat it, because one cannot combat something which is not accepted as something which really exists.

Once the true phenomenon is denied, or more correctly, it is defined in such a way that its essential characteristics are unknown, the most characteristic profiles and the most serious problematic which it reveals, the broadest spaces are opened to give it weight.

In effect, the changes in the military high command which were carried out last November constituted the most explicit official support behind paramilitarism, and, along the way, an energetic backing for impunity. To prove this, it is only necessary to look rapidly at the lists of the MAS, promulgated by Procurador Jimenez Gomez, to those of the "Triple A," to the numerous confessions referred to above of outstanding figures who have been shamed by paramilitarism and numerous measures left half done by the judicial and disciplinary powers, thanks to the effective mechanisms of impunity already described.

But the Samper government has wished to go even further: it has rapidly provided "legal" status to paramilitarism, reformulated as "Communitary Associations of Rural Vigilance."

The communique issued by the office of the president on December 13, 1994, "legalized" the elements which constitute paramilitarism, not just permitting it or tolerating it by means of implicit mechanisms, groups of armed civilians, but rather creating and giving them "legal life," sustaining them in a supposed "defensive" legitimation (like the "Autodefensas" originated in Puerto Boyaca and expanded throughout the entire national territory) (see Communique No. 7 sub-paragraph b); coordinated by the Public Forces (Communique No. 7, sub-paragraph c); provided with arms by the Public Forces (Communique No. 7, sub-paragraph e) and financed jointly by the public sector and the private sector (Communique, No. 6). All of the parameters of paramilitarism were reedited there and would acquire, now truly, "legal" status.

The foundation for a reactivation of paramilitarism, having been laid down, and paramilitarism not now being secret, the euphoria was not long in coming. The first half of 1995 has seen the overflowing euphoria of the paramilitary groups (and it is now known that their euphoria is bloody).

The document of the First Summit of Autodefensas of Colombia, which took place at the beginning of 1995 in some part of the country, stated that "fortunately the autodefensas have been revived in the national territory, with a common identity, without leaving the "antisubversive" line" (page 49).

This same document affirms that "no self-defense group allied with the

> autodefensas of Colombia, will return to demobilize its men and it will not fall into the same error as Fidel Castano, who having been convinced that he had eradicated the guerrillas from the zone where he operated, and that the Armed Forces could control it and he demobilized his organization for a while. During this space of time the Armed Forces could not maintain control of the region....And for this reason Fidel Castano found himself obliged to reactivate his self-defense forces" (page 55).

Effectively that part of Uraba in Antioquia and in Cordoba returned in 1995 to be a prisoner of paramilitarism. Disappearances, massacres, assassinations, torture and forced displacement of entire communities were recorded in the report of national and international NGOs which visited the region in April of 1995.

Putumayo, Cesar, Catatumbo and the Province of Ocana, Meta, the Middle Magdalena, the South of Bolivar, Valle and Cauca, Boyaca, Casanare and Arauca, Caqueta and the coffee-growing axis, the Northeast and Southeast of Antioquia, several zones of Santander and the popular communes of Bogota, Medellin and Cali, have experienced in the last several months an impressive increase in paramilitarism.

In Villavicencio, a convention was called together in the meeting place of the Departmental Assembly in the month of March and it reiterated in diverse tones the former goal of "extermination of the Patriotic Union." Since February, the threats against the Civic Committee of Human Rights of Meta have been multiplied, obliging it to close its offices and move them to Bogota last May.

The cited document of the Summit says that "it was agreed to group together all of the existing self-defense organizations (Autodefensas) in the country which possess a transparent place in the counterinsurgency struggle based around the organization of autodefensas of Colombia, with the principal mission of combating subversion in the national territory...." It is reported that they were organized in structures such as GRAU (the Urban Self-Defense Group), GRIN (Intelligence Groups) and GRAP (Political Support Groups) and that "it was approved to continue considering those political and union personalities (cuadros) of the extreme left as military targets...."

Whoever reads the mentioned document, above all the chapter on the Armed Forces (pages 18-38), will have little doubt left about its military authorship.

Nor is there any doubt about the reactivation of paramilitarism which has been registered under the Samper government, and upon reading it with the backdrop of its historical development, illuminated by the coincident and overwhelming confessions of its authorized exponents, no one will doubt that what exists is an unyielding Policy of State which is devouring our martyred country.

A Call to Action:
What You Can Do

There are many ways you can help to change the terrible reality of Colombia. Here are some of them.

1. If you are a member of a Peace and Justice organization, put the situation in Colombia in your organization's agenda.

2. Start a committee to provide solidarity for those who work for peace and justice in Colombia.

3. Contact your Congresspeople, the president and secretary of state. Ask them to encourage Colombian officials to protect human rights, end impunity for the abuses, and to see that the Colombian system of justice is applied fairly. Encourage U.S. government officials to hold public hearings on the human rights situation in Colombia.

4. Join a delegation to Colombia to get a first hand view of the situation there and to provide support for those whose lives are threatened because of their defense of human dignity and human rights.

5. Inform the press in your community and nationally about the tragic situation in Colombia and urge them to keep writing about it until change occurs.

6. Begin a sister community project between your community and a community in Colombia which is facing the dangers outlined in this book.

7. Subscribe to our "Action on Colombia" newsletter and follow the Colombia Support Network page on the World Wide Web.

For assistance with any of these actions, contact
The Colombia Support Network
P.O. Box 1505
Madison, WI 53701-1505
Fax: 608-255-6621
http://www.igc.apc.org/csn/csn.html

Index

About the Author

Father Giraldo was born in Colombia in 1944. He studied Philosophy and Theology at the Universidad Javeriana en Bogota and then Social Sciences at the University of Paris in France. He worked as a parish priest at a popular neighborhood in Bogota; then as a researcher at the prestigious Centro de Investigacion y Educacion Popular (CINEP) in Bogota at the Department of Urban Affairs and at the Office for Human Rights.

In 1988 he became Executive Director of the Comision Intercongrecacional de Justicia y Paz, from the Conferencia de Religiosos de Colombia which is an umbrella organization of more than 55 Catholic Religious Congregations such as Jesuits, Franciscans, and Salesians.

He has also been the Secretary for Latin America of the Permanent Tribunal of the People's for the Session on Impunity for Crimes against Humanity in Latin America (1989-91).

He has published in *La Reivindicacion Urbana* (CINEP, 1986), and in the series "El Camino de la Niebla" (The Foggy Road), 3 volumes on cases of impunity in Colombia (Justicia y Paz). He lives in Colombia.